HOME DECORATING

HAMLYN PRACTICAL DIY GUIDES

HOME DECORATING

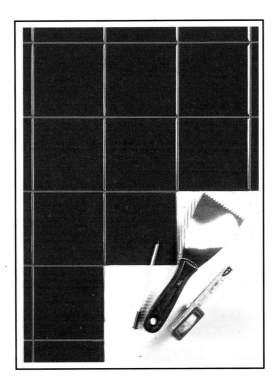

Tony Wilkins

HAMLYN

ACKNOWLEDGEMENTS

Editor:
Carolyn Pyrah

•

Technical Consultant:
Mike Trier

•

Art Editor:
Pedro Prá-Lopez

•

Design:
Vicky Pacey

•

Special Photography:
Jon Bouchier

•

Illustration:
Irwin Technical

•

Picture Research:
Rachel Duffield, Frances Topp

•

Production Controller:
Jenny May

•

First published in 1990 by
The Hamlyn Publishing Group Limited
a division of
The Octopus Publishing Group
Michelin House
81 Fulham Road
LONDON SW3 6RB

© The Hamlyn Publishing Group Limited
1990

ISBN 0-600-56466-5

Produced by Mandarin Offset
Printed and bound in Hong Kong

The Publishers thank the following for providing the photographs in this book:
Acorn Decorating Products 20 top; Aquaseal 45 top right; Armstrong 78; Blue Hawk Artex 12; Michael Boys Syndication 8 left, 9 below right, 54 top left, 68 left, 68 below right, 74 below, 85, 86 top left, 86 below left, 87 below left, 91 top left; Camera Press 6; Crown Decorative Projects Ltd 13 top left; Crown Paints 76, 81, 92 right; Cuprinol 45 below left, centre and right; English Abrasives and Chemicals 30 left; Eureka Products Ltd 77; Eurostudio Design 68 top right; Evo-Stick 45 top centre; P.C. Henderson Ltd 54 below; Heuga (UK) Ltd 84; Houses and Interiors 9 top right, 30 right, 42, 43 below, 44 top left and right, 53, 55; ICI paints 57; Nitromors 43 top left and right; North Western Lead Company (Hyde) Ltd 92 top and below left; Octopus Group Picture Library/Dave King 29 below right; Osborne and Little plc 11 left; Ruflette 86 centre right, 89 below right; Snowcem PMC Ltd 44 below; Sterling Roncraft 47, 54 top right; Swish Products Ltd 88, 89 top right, Turner Wallcoverings 33 top; Vencel Resil Ltd 37 below; Westco Floorcoverings Ltd 83 left; Elizabeth Whiting Associates 3, 8 right, 11 right, 75, 86 top right, 87 below right, 89 below left; /Michael Crockett 91 below left; /Michael Dunne 9 below right, 70 top, 87 top right, 87 below centre, 93 top right; /Clive Helm 9 left, 87 top left; /Ann Kelley 29 below left; /Tom Leighton 93 top left; /Neil Lorimer 13 top right, 36 top right, 90; /Michael Nicholson 86 below right; /Spike Powell 35 left, 41 left, 69, 91 top right, 91 below right; /Tim Street-Porter 91 below centre; /Ron Sutherland 93 below left; /Jerry Tubby 32 left, 74 top, 89 top left, 93 below right; Willoughby Stewart Associates 28, 29 top, 45 top left.

The Publishers thank the following companies for supplying merchandise for special photography:
Boyden & Co. Ltd 73; Muraspec Textured Wallcoverings Ltd 9 bottom right, 30 top left, 31 top right, 32, 33 bottom left; John Oliver Wallpapers 68 (beige border); Reed Harris Ltd 37; Arthur Sanderson & Son Ltd 8 bottom left, 8 top, 10 centre right (fabric), 10 right (fabric), 31 centre left, 31 right, 68 (blue flowered border); Sue Stowell Ltd 9 top left, 10 (from left, last 2 rolls of wallcovering); Turners Wallcoverings 33 right; Warner & Son Ltd 8/9 bottom centre, 9 top right, 10 left (fabric), 10 centre left (fabric), 10 (from left, first 5 rolls of wallcovering), 30 top right, 31 centre right, 31 bottom, 68 (except beige and blue flowered borders).

With special thanks to Sarah Bouchier, Dave Kinross and Philip Oakley. Subjects for photography supplied by Sainsbury's Homebase.

CONTENTS

INTRODUCTION
PAGE 6

COLOUR, PATTERN AND TEXTURE
PAGE 8

TOOLS FOR THE JOB
PAGE 14

MATERIALS
PAGE 28

PREPARATION
PAGE 39

PAINTING
PAGE 48

WALLCOVERINGS
PAGE 58

TILING
PAGE 69

FLOORING
PAGE 76

FITTINGS AND FIXTURES
PAGE 85

GLOSSARY
PAGE 94

INDEX
PAGE 95

INTRODUCTION

You have now decided to change the look of your home – whether it is for the first time in a new home, or whether you are adding a new lease of life to familiar territory. Decorating allows you to stamp your individual character on each room, transforming it with the textures, colours and patterns of your choice.

DESIGN CO-ORDINATION

It is not always easy to decide on a scheme, so spend time looking for inspiration in books, magazines, and by collecting colour charts and fabric swatches that appeal. The first chapter will give you guidelines – as you read it keep in mind all the time the type of house or flat you live in.

Buy the best materials you can afford: inferior paints are less durable and cut-price wallpapers are often difficult to hang. Make sure you have all the materials you need before you start work.

For jobs you will only tackle rarely, you may prefer to hire equipment. Professional equipment is available which can take a lot of the hard work out of a task. You must, however, familiarize yourself with the equipment prior to use.

FIRST-CLASS RESULTS

Have you the right tools for the job? Good-quality tools make for light work and ensure a fine finish. On the following pages is a checklist, covering both tools for general repair work and those you will need for decorating.

Careful preparation is vital for best results. It is a good idea to work out an order of work, building in plenty of time for preparatory jobs which must be done before decorating starts. These may be major tasks, such as installing a new fireplace, or dirty jobs, like channelling a wall for new cable runs for wall lights. Some you may wish to do yourself, for others you may prefer to employ an expert. Any messy jobs which would spoil new decoration need to be tackled first.

HOME SAFETY

Keep safety in mind at all times – both indoors and out-of-doors. Use safe access equipment, avoid potentially dangerous tools, and wear protective clothing. Safety precautions are given in early chapters.

The main advantage you have over the professional as you work is time. Break your work into easily manageable projects which you can complete in the time available, and you will work more efficiently and find decorating more rewarding.

Home Decorating covers all of these points in detail and many more. Whether you use it for step-by-step reference, browse through it for inspiration, or learn an easier way of tackling a job you have done before, we wish you every success with your decorating.

COLOUR, PATTERN AND TEXTURE

Your first move towards decorating any room should be to decide what character and mood you want the room to express. Do you want it to be light and airy or restful and cosy? Colour has a great influence on mood.

How will your furniture and furnishings fit in? They must influence the scheme you choose. For example, if you have a patterned three-piece suite and curtains to match, you may not want heavily-patterned walls. Plain ones will act as a contrast.

Start by collecting samples of fabric, paint colour cards and pieces of carpet and work out a colour scheme by selecting items from each category which go together.

COLOUR

It does not take much imagination to realize how strong an effect colour has on us. Imagine sleeping in a bright red bedroom, or eating breakfast in a bright green kitchen! When selecting colours, take into account the aspect of the room being decorated: do the windows face north, south, east or west? Rooms looking to the north will receive little sunlight and tend to feel colder, while those facing south may feel over-warm. Rooms facing east or west will vary according to the time of day. With this in mind, you may wish to add warmth or coolness by your choice of colour. A bright room will be able to take darker shades than a duller, north-facing room.

You can use colour to seemingly affect the size of a room. Dark brown in a very small room will make it seem even smaller, whereas pale blue will make it seem larger. Similarly dark colours will seem to lower a ceiling, and light ones raise it.

Colour effects

As a general guide, use reds and oranges for warmth – but too much is disturbing. Use blues and white for coolness, though these colours are not always relaxing. Pastel greens are calming, but vivid greens can be unsettling. Browns and rusts are cosy and restful. Pale yellow is uplifting, though too much of it could make you feel dizzy. The blush white shades are popular for subtle backgrounds: with these, splashes of brighter colour can be added elsewhere with less risk that colours will clash.

Your choice of lighting will also affect the mood of the room. Lamplight will generally lend warmth. If you wish to tone down a colour, try lighting it with its complementary hue. For example, a blue wall suffused in orange lamplight will appear to be a duller shade of blue than it actually is.

A cold room can be transformed by the use of warm colours like apricot, red, rust or peach. Here, a north-facing room has been decorated in a strong terracotta, but pale tones can be just as effective. As well as the colour of the paint, a wallcovering or fabric, take into account wood tones. Natural wood will add warmth

The colours of the sea, aqua, blue, turquoise and white, are cool, relaxing and ideal for use in a south-facing room. In this bedroom shades of blue and white set the mood, while minimal furnishings and the openweave cane chair create a feeling of space. Add a touch of warmth with deep-coloured accessories

Pale colours can considerably increase the apparent size of a room. Apart from tricks with light wall and ceiling colours, bear in mind that low furniture will also create more space. Pick fabrics in plain pastels or a mix of muted tones (see left)

In rooms used mainly in the evening you can afford to use strong colours that are enriched by the warm glow of electric lamplight. In the corner of this room, the tones of the accessories and the gilt picture frame suggest opulence

In large rooms bright primary colours and bold patterns can be used to great effect. This living room, with its golden, sponged walls, provides constant sunlight. Even the books add a patchwork of bright colour. A large room is also the ideal place to show off a decorative rug. Accessories and flowers enhance the summer theme

Soft greens provide a restful background reminiscent of the peaceful countryside. Science has proved that colour has a strong influence on us: red has successfully been used to stimulate children, and green to introduce harmony in stressful surroundings. Here low, light-coloured furniture also creates a sense of space

PATTERN

When using patterned fabrics and wallcoverings, aim to co-ordinate pattern, colour and texture in a pleasing arrangement with the furnishings and dimensions of the room, taking into account the function of the room and age of your home. The resulting image you create will reflect your taste and personality.

Patterns must be chosen with an awareness for the finished effect. A patterned swatch of wallpaper may appeal to you on a small scale, but could look dominating on all four walls of a room.

Do not be afraid to experiment. Try mixing stripes with floral designs, small and large prints, contrasting and complementary colours. Look for inspiration in books and magazines. Aim to achieve a balanced effect, carrying colour and design themes through a room. You might like to base the colours of a patterned wallpaper on the colour of existing upholstery in a room. Whatever you decide upon, your aim first and foremost should be to create an environment in which you feel comfortable.

Choosing a focal point

Decide on the focal point of the room, and work your design ideas around it. This may be a period fireplace, a rug, or there may be other features you wish to enhance. A large bay window seat overlooking a flower garden could be emphasized by adding a window seat and curtains in matching floral fabric. If you make the most of attractive features, you will find that less attractive areas recede.

The scale of the pattern in relation to the size of room is important. Small rooms generally call for smaller patterns, for a large pattern will tend to dominate in a small area. Conversely, large rooms usually call for larger patterns. Very delicate patterns can become just a blur at a distance, sometimes producing a dull effect.

Pattern direction will determine whether or not a room looks taller or wider. You may need to see an area of the wallcovering before you get a real feel for the pattern direction.

Patterns with a vertical theme make a room look taller, and might work well in a room with a low

Pick wallpapers and fabrics in patterns and colours which improve the dimensions of the surroundings. Add height with a vertically-striped wallcovering or create space with small, pale patterns. Bold patterns catch attention

ceiling. However, never use vertical stripes if walls are out of true. You will only draw attention to the fault.

'Lowering' a ceiling

If you choose to have a patterned ceiling paper, be especially careful to consider the effect it will have. If you wish to 'lower' a very high ceiling, a good trick is to use a dark patterned ceiling covering.

Horizontal patterns help to bring down the apparent level of a ceiling, but also tend to elongate the room. Avoid them if you have an uneven or sloping ceiling or you will highlight the problem.

Diagonal patterns can look confusing in unusually-shaped rooms. A random pattern creates few problems and makes matching easy.

*You may want to create a modern look or prefer to recreate the past. **Right:** Stripes and a splattered paper bring traditional surroundings up-to-date. **Below:** Florals are reminiscent of a country cottage*

MIRROR MAGIC

Cleverly used, mirrors can be an exciting decorative aid. Use mirror glass to give a feeling of spaciousness in small rooms. In the bathroom, a wall of mirror will seem to double the size of the room, while using sheet mirror as a bath panel will seemingly feed the carpet under the bath. A small bedroom will benefit from mirror doors on wardrobes, and a dark passageway will benefit from a wall of mirror which will reflect any available light.

Apart from sheet mirror, flexible mosaic tiles are also available. They look good in alcoves, backing shelving or as a feature under cabinets. If you are thinking of using tinted glass, get a sample first and experiment to see if you get the desired effect before ordering any quantity.

Remember that mirrors used in kitchens and bathrooms need to be damp-resistant – check this when ordering them.

TEXTURE

Adding texture to a surface has two main values, one decorative and the other cosmetic. Texture enhances decoration by making flat surfaces look more interesting, but must be related to the light source. If you decorate a wall which is at right angles to a window with a textured surface, you will enhance the effect of the texture by introducing light and shade. Wall lights will have a similar effect on a textured surface. If you light a texture face on, it will make it look flat. From a cosmetic point of view, textures allow you to disguise uneven or irregular surfaces. You will find a whole range of wallcoverings offering different textures. Here are a few:

Embossed These wallcoverings have a texture pressed into them during manufacture, so that they are raised on the decorative side and hollow on the reverse. Some are coloured, others are for emulsion coating. Be careful when papering not to press the embossed surface flat.

Wood chip These consist of two layers of paper with chips of wood sandwiched between them. They are for emulsion coating.

Blown vinyl Vinyl is expanded on the surface of the paper during manufacture, providing a textured surface which recovers if squashed. It has some insulation value and provides a smooth backing.

Imitation Imitation brick, stone, tiling, panelling and planking effects come both naturally coloured and plain for painting, and are reproduced by the roll.

Slips Pieces of brick and stone are available, some moulded from concrete or plaster and others made of the real thing.

Textured Paint

This special paint or compound is spread in a thick layer on walls. It also provides a simple way of hiding joins in plasterboard ceilings, and of hiding any visible fixing nails.

A word of caution: textured paint is a permanent form of decoration, and is difficult to remove. It may be better to apply a textured paper, which can easily be stripped if you want a change at a later date.

Application is best by paint roller, as the material is laid on thickly and the surface roughed up by the roller. Special textured rollers are available, but you can also experiment after application with various materials which change the texture. A wad of rag, decorating sponge, special comb or brush all produce different effects. It is wise to experiment and practise the finish you decide upon before starting work.

Special roller sleeves allow you to create a range of diamond, diagonal and bark effects plus many other patterns, by running the roller over the wet surface

Use the flat of a paint brush in overlapping strokes to create the look of old and uneven plaster. Clean the brush regularly to retain the texture

A rubber-bristled stippling brush can be patted up and down on a surface to provide a rough, even texture. By twisting the brush you can also create swirls. It is best to experiment first

Overlapping fan shapes, basket weave and many other repeat patterns can be created with this special toothed tool or with a comb. These patterns are the most difficult to create, so practise first

Heavily-embossed borders in traditional designs help blend antique and reproduction furniture with modern surroundings

Ideal for covering a poorly plastered wall, tongue and groove boards can be used to blend old with new in an extension

1. Cork floor tiles
2. Hexagonal quarry tiles
3. Embossed wallpaper
4. Quarry tiles
5. Brick slips
6. Blown vinyl border
7. Quarry tiles in a range of colours
8. Hessian wallcovering
9. Stone slips
10. Pine panelling
11. Parquet floor tiles
12. A range of carpet tiles

TOOLS FOR THE JOB

Having the right tools for the job greatly simplifies the task in hand and ensures the best possible finish. Some tools may be expensive, but the cost must be weighed against the money you will save by not paying someone to do the work. Always buy the best tools. Since good, well-cared-for tools will last, they are also an investment.

Sharp scissors and knives will give a cleaner cut and will be safer to use. In the main do not buy made-up tool kits. They often contain quite a number of tools you will never use. Be selective in your choice of tools, governed by the work you plan to do.

Clean tools immediately after use. A wipe with an oily rag will ensure metal surfaces stay rust-free. Never let sharp tools rub against each other. It is the most common cause of blunted cutting edges.

Learn how to use tools correctly, keeping your hands well away from the direction of any cut. Wherever possible, clamp work so that both hands are free to hold the tool correctly.

Always unplug power tools when not in use, and store out of reach of children. Wear protective clothing where recommended. (*See page 26, Protective Clothing.*)

A soft hold-all is best for transporting tools. Wooden tool boxes are heavy and cumbersome.

A BASIC TOOL KIT

The following tools will be useful for most household jobs. Specific tools for painting, papering and tiling appear in following chapters.

Workmate (portable workbench) This can also be used for firmly holding work, is suitable to stand on or use as one of two trestles.

Steel rule For marking a straight line and for use as a cutting guide.

Metre rule Plastic ones are lightweight.

Tenon saw For fine cutting, 255mm (10in) 13pt. (The 'point' refers to the number of teeth per 25mm of blade).

GP (General Purpose) saw This is for cutting metal or wood. It is ideal for sawing secondhand timber or joinery containing nails or screws.

Mini hacksaw For cutting metal.

Cross-cut handsaw 560mm (22in) 10pt. This is made for larger timbers.

Cross-slot screwdriver Made for Supadriv screws.

Single slot screwdriver Ratchet-action is the advantage of this screwdriver.

Electricians' screwdriver This has an insulated handle, just in case you touch a live wire.

Clamps For holding work, 100mm and 200mm (4in and 8in).

Power drill (*See page 17, Using Power Tools.*)

Set of twist drills and masonry drills These drills are not interchangeable.

Self-grip wrench (Mole) This snaplocks on to objects, leaving hands free.

Fine nose pliers

Pincers For pulling nails.

Craft knife With disposable blades.

1. Pincers, 2. File for metal, 3. Electricians' screwdriver, 4. Ratchet-action single slot screwdriver, 5. Cross slot screwdriver, 6. Soft-faced hammer, 7. Pin hammer, 8. Claw hammer, 9. General purpose saw, 10. Surform, 11. Cross-cut saw, 12. Metre rule, 13. Cordless screwdriver, 14. Cordless drill, 15. Mini hacksaw, 16. Self-grip wrench, fine nose pliers and an adjustable spanner in tool carrier, 17. Adjustable clamp, 18. Tenon saw, 19. Bevel-edge chisels, 20. Blade cover to protect chisels, 21. Retractable steel rule, 22. Try square, 23. Tile cutter for thin tiles, 24. Spirit level (long ones are more accurate), 25. Disposable-blade craft knife, 26. Hot melt glue gun

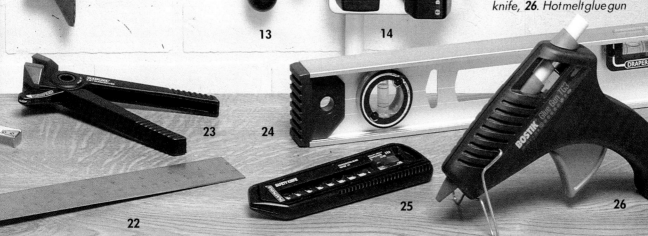

Adjustable spanner 24mm (¹⁵/₁₆in) opening.
Chisels Choose the bevel edge type. Sizes vary: 6mm, 12mm, 19mm and 25mm (¼in, ½in, ¾in, 1in).
Claw hammer The claw draws nails.
Pin hammer Use this for small nails.
Spirit level This need not be longer than 800mm (32in). Generally the longer it is the more accurate it is.
Glass cutter
Soft-face hammer Useful for hitting metal and wood surfaces, it leaves no mark.

Try-square For marking right angles.
File For smoothing metal 12mm (½in) half-round.
Steel measuring tape This has a dual metric/imperial reading.
Glue gun Filled with sticks of adhesive and sealant, this is useful for quick repair work.
Staple gun A quick way of fixing thin sheet plywood, hardboard, fabrics and so on is with staples.
Shaping tool Surform 225mm (9in).
Large hacksaw and spare blades 300mm (12in).
Tool carrier

Storing Tools

Make sure that tools are stored in a dry place when not in use. A garage is not an ideal place if a wet car is likely to be parked there occasionally.

To store tools, cover a free wall with a large board of MDF (Medium Density Fireboard) or pegboard lifted away from the wall. (If you do not lift it away from the wall the pegs will not go through the board.) Use suitable clips to hold the tools to the board. You could also draw silhouettes around each tool, so that if a tool is missing it will be obvious.

1. Pasting brush for wallpapering
2. Paint and wallpaper scrapers: two, one wide and one narrow, are useful
3. Paintbrushes: four in a range of sizes will cover most jobs
4. Shavehook for removing paint from

around mouldings
5. Rollers: foam or mohair roller for smooth surfaces, a longer pile one for uneven surfaces
6. Staple gun
7. Retractable steel rule

8. Wallpapering scissors
9. Disposable-blade craft knife
10. Glasspaper and sanding pad
11. Template former for reproducing complex shapes
12. Paint pads

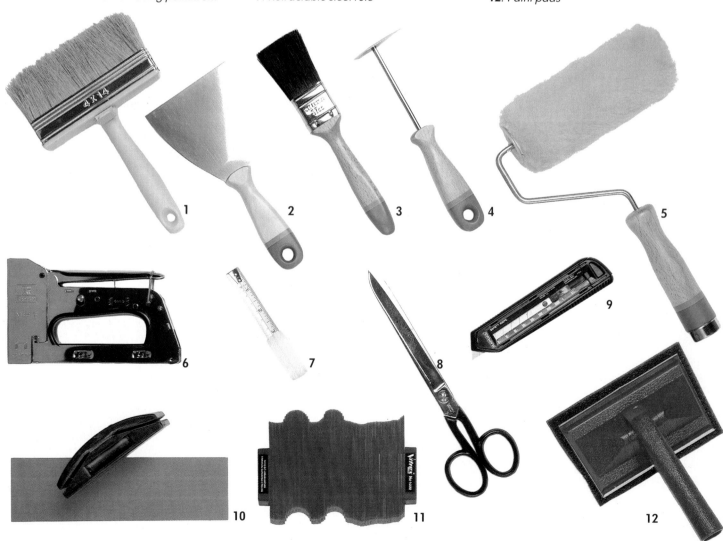

USING POWER TOOLS

Power tools are a great help in making work easier and results more accurate. Choose integral tools rather than a basic drill with lots of attachments. Tools specifically designed for a job will have the right range of speeds, be well balanced and easy to use.

Extension Cable

For jobs away from a power supply you will need a good extension cable drum. Cordless, rechargeable tools are less powerful but are good back-up to standard power tools. They are also safe to use out-of-doors.

Safety

As a safety precaution for mains-operated power tools, use an RCCB (residual current circuit breaker). This will cut off the power supply in the event of any fault or accident.

Jig saw Invaluable for general cutting of timber and sheet materials, the best jig saw will have a reciprocal action blade and blowing action to clear the cutting line. Scroll action is another refinement, enabling you to make tight curved cuts by turning the blade and not the whole tool.

Circular saw Useful for cutting sheet materials and timber in a straight line, this is not so versatile as the jig saw. Blades are available for cutting different materials.
File sander Resembling a thin belt sander, it is useful for both shaping and finishing work.
Belt sander This is useful for sanding large surfaces. Unless you do a lot of work, it is probably best hired.
Steam stripper A domestic one-hand steam stripper is available for removing stubborn wallcoverings. A larger version can be hired.
Spray gun *See page 21*.

1. Foam drum sander. Unlike a circular sanding disc this does not leave sanding rings and can be used on both flat and shaped surfaces
2. Sanding disc with glasspaper
3. Wire brush attachment

4. Wire cup brush for removing rust
5. Coarse, medium and fine grades of glasspaper
6. Orbital sander. This gives a smooth finish to wood
7. Twist drill and masonry drill kits. Twist

drills are unsuitable for masonry use
8. Power drill. Optional hammer action is useful for drilling masonry
9. Key for releasing and changing drill bits and accessories
10. Hot air stripper for stripping paintwork

TOOLS FOR PAINTING

How you decide to apply paint is largely a matter of personal choice. Good quality brushes are often used in conjunction with the paint-roller, a tool specially developed for the amateur to apply emulsion paints. The paint pad is less widely used, despite its advantages (*see page 20*). Unlike the roller, it does not cause paint to spatter.

There are a few special tools you will need as well. These include: shave hooks (pear-shaped and triangular) and flexible scrapers (wide and narrow) for removing old paint; masking tape for protecting surfaces not to be painted; paint shield in metal or plastic to contain paint within the area being painted; tack or tacky rag to pick up fine dust; lint-free rags for wiping up

(clean old handkerchiefs are ideal); paint stirrers – you can insert one type of paint stirrer in the chuck of a power tool; paint kettles, in which to dispense paint for painting. A paint kettle will ensure that the bulk of your paint is kept free from contamination, as you can put a little paint at a time in the kettle. It also facilitates carrying (for example if you are painting the top of a wall from a ladder), as not all tins of paint have handles.

Brushes

For a really fine finish, insist on quality brushes composed of Chinese hog bristle. Many attempts have been made to replace hog bristle with synthetic fibre, with very poor results. Price can sometimes affect

the quantity of bristles you get in a brush stock (base of the handle). Often the difference in price is directly related to the bulk – and the more bristles your brush has, the more paint it will hold.

Some jobs, however, do not call for such high quality: there is no need to use your best brushes for applying preservatives to fencing or masonry paint to a wall. Choose the size of brush to suit the surface you have to paint, and use your widest brushes for large surface areas.

If they are well cared for, brushes improve with use. They shed loose bristles and the tips become nicely rounded. Start a brush on primer and undercoat, then use it for fine finishing as it ages. A useful range of brush sizes would include an

angled 18mm (¾in) cutting-in brush and 12mm, 25mm, 50mm and 100mm or 125mm (½in, 1in, 2in and 4in or 5in) brushes. Keep special brushes for masonry paints, preservatives, and protective coatings separate from fine finish brushes.

Rollers

Used with a paint tray, the roller offers an easy way of applying paint to large, flat areas and does not leave defined brush strokes. It is best for applying water-based paints, which easily clean off the roller. If solid emulsion is used, lift the roller direct from the container. Some brush cleaners can damage a roller, destroying the adhesive bond of roller to core. The following are the main types of roller:

Foam A good general purpose roller, but it does not provide the finest of finishes and rough surfaces will tear the foam. Usually it is easy to clean as the foam sleeve can be slipped from the core.

Mohair This has a very close pile on a hard roller, and will give a fine finish to smooth, flat surfaces. It is not suitable for textured surfaces.

Shaggy pile This roller has a deep, floppy pile, making it ideal for textured surfaces. A special tough variety is available for use on exterior rough rendered surfaces. Inside it can be used to apply textured paint.

Radiator roller This is a special tool comprising a thin, deep-pile roller on a long wire handle so you can paint behind radiators, pipes and hard-to-reach places.

SOAKING BRUSHES

Never stand brushes in water. It expands the stock (base of the handle), rusts the metal ferrule and deforms the tip. If you wish to leave gloss-loaded brushes to soak, use white spirit in a jar. Drill a hole through the brush handle, push stiff wire through the hole and rest it on the rim of the jar so the brush is suspended in the white spirit.

While taking a short break, load brushes with paint and wrap them tightly in kitchen foil to prevent air reaching the bristles.

If bristles become hard, you can soften them with a proprietary brush restorer but, when clean, do not use them again for top coats.

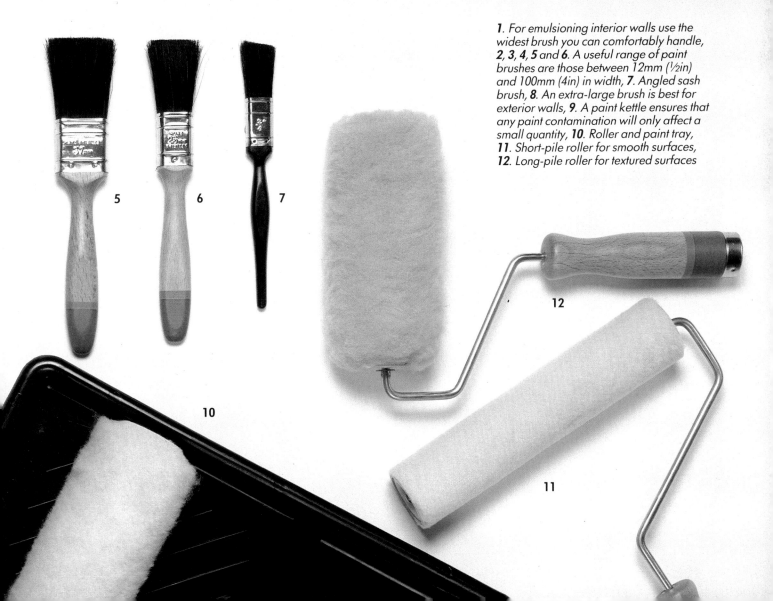

1. For emulsioning interior walls use the widest brush you can comfortably handle, 2, 3, 4, 5 and 6. A useful range of paint brushes are those between 12mm (½in) and 100mm (4in) in width, 7. Angled sash brush, 8. An extra-large brush is best for exterior walls, 9. A paint kettle ensures that any paint contamination will only affect a small quantity, 10. Roller and paint tray, 11. Short-pile roller for smooth surfaces, 12. Long-pile roller for textured surfaces

Paint Pads

A paint pad consists of a fine mohair pile stuck to a layer of foam to make it flexible. This in turn is bonded to a metal or plastic handle.

Paint pads come in a variety of sizes from 25mm to 150mm (1in to 6in), and all are light and easy to use. Some have a hollow handle to take the end of a broom; this makes it possible to tackle the main part of a wall or ceiling without using steps.

The pad is suitable for smooth and textured surfaces, but should not be used on rough finishes as they will damage the mohair. A 25mm (1in) paintbrush is useful for finishing edges.

It is vital to clean pads as soon as you have finished work. Use pads with water-based materials and clean them with water, as proprietary cleaners often attack the adhesive holding the mohair to the foam. However, a pad can give a very fine finish when you are gloss-painting flush doors.

Specialist Brushes

Apart from standard brushes, you will find some designed for specific jobs – not all jobs require such a high quality bristle. These include:

Distemper brush Although distemper is not commonly used, the brush is still useful for painting large areas, applying wallpaper paste or

Left: Paint pads produce a smooth finish on walls and ceilings. **Below: 1.** *Small paint pad,* **2.** *Pad with angled handle for awkward areas,* **3.** *Large pad,* **4** *and* **5.** *Long-handled radiator brushes*

wetting down surfaces. Usually it has a mixture of bristle, fibre and synthetic filament.

Creosote brush Suitable for all preservatives, it often has synthetic bristles and is coarse in texture.

Dusting brush As the name implies, this brush is used for dusting off surfaces prior to painting but after rubbing down. It is usually made of bristle, horse hair and fibre. You could use an ordinary paint brush instead as long as you keep it just for that job.

Masonry paint brush A thick brush of mainly artificial fibres, this holds a lot of paint. A soft dustpan brush is a good substitute.

Rubberized paint brush This wide, full-bodied brush of coarse, artificial fibres is disposable. It may be sold as a creosote brush.

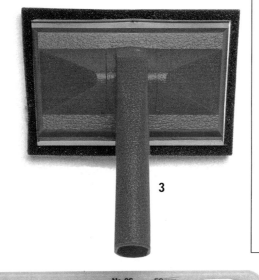

1   2   3

No.26   50mm
RADIATOR BRUSH
MADE IN SWEDEN

4   5

CLEANING BRUSHES

Most paint cans advise you what to use for cleaning brushes. All are designed to be used while the brush is still soft.

Water-based paints Clean brushes with water as soon as possible.

Oil-based paints Use a proprietary brush cleaner then rinse in water, or use white spirit, then wash in warm, soapy water. Some paints recommend using only powder detergent and hand-hot water.

Enamels Use special enamel thinners or white spirit.

Varnishes Use white spirit, followed by warm, soapy water, then rinse brushes.

Cellulose Use special cellulose thinners.

Rubberized paints Special solvents are recommended.

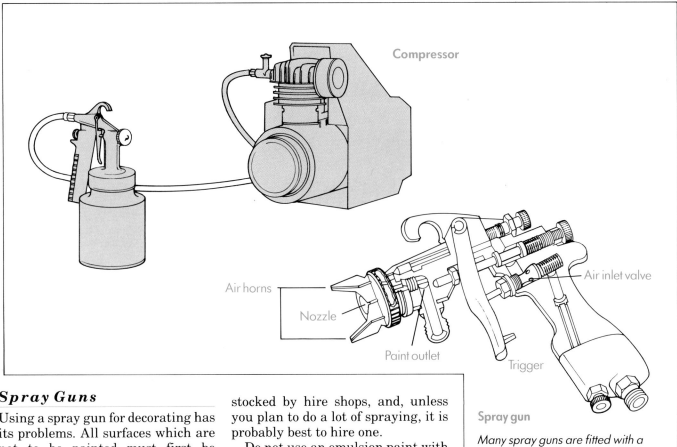

Compressor

Air horns

Nozzle

Paint outlet

Trigger

Air inlet valve

Spray gun

Many spray guns are fitted with a cap with projecting horns, which mixes air with paint externally. The horns direct air to produce a fan of spray paint, rather than a single jet

Spray Guns

Using a spray gun for decorating has its problems. All surfaces which are not to be painted must first be masked – and you must be very careful that spray does not drift. Outside it may reach as far as neighbours' parked cars or homes. There are two distinct types of spray equipment:

Airless This is an electrically operated gun. The airless gun has an in-built high pressure pump which forces paint from a fine nozzle, breaking the paint into a fine spray.

This is probably the best gun for DIY use as no air is present to spread the over-spray around. However, anything but the thinnest of coats of paint will run (known as curtaining), so it is wise to practise before tackling the real thing. The nozzle can be adjusted to cover small or wide areas.

Compressed air Here, a separate compressor feeds air to the gun, where it is mixed with paint before emerging at the nozzle. This gun gives finer control of spray, and thin coats can be achieved quite easily. Compressed air guns are usually

stocked by hire shops, and, unless you plan to do a lot of spraying, it is probably best to hire one.

Do not use an emulsion paint with a spray gun as it tends to clog the nozzle very quickly. Cellulose paint is easy to use as it can be readily thinned. An oil-based paint can be used, but it must also be thinned to prevent clogging. Clean the apparatus well straight after use, before the paint dries in the nozzle.

There is a special technique for spraying a surface which takes practice. Hold the gun with the nozzle about 20cm (8in) from the surface to be coated, then move the gun parallel with the surface. Keep spraying just off the end of the surface then switch the gun off. Never swing the gun in an arc, or the quantity of paint applied over any one area will vary considerably.

Apply only very thin, even coats. Allow each coat to harden before the next is applied. Keep applying thin layers of paint until the correct density is reached – in this way you will avoid curtaining. If the gun splutters, it is probably due to hardened paint blocking the nozzle.

CAREFUL SPRAYING

A fine mist of spray in the air can be a menace – both indoors and out. Take small objects, like a Lloyd loom chair, into an area free from wind, and make up a simple booth from cardboard so that any over-spray is contained.

With larger areas – such as a garage door – use masking tape and newspaper to mask off all nearby areas not to be painted. Choose a still day, and remove any vehicles parked close by.

When working in confined areas, wear goggles and a simple face mask. If cellulose is used, work in a well-ventilated area to allow fumes to disperse. Remember the fumes are highly inflammable.

TOOLS FOR WALLPAPERING

You will need to add a few more special tools when you start papering. The following is a checklist:

Pasting table Buy a sturdy pasting table. Alternatively you could use a flush door laid over trestles. It is always useful to have a table, even if you are working with a ready-pasted wallcovering.

Bucket Use a clean plastic one, with string tied across the top on which to rest the paste brush.

Scissors You will need a pair of long decorating scissors and a small pair for trimming.

Craft knife You would use this with a straight-edge or cutting guide to trim vinyls and heavy papers. Scissors are best with thin, wet paper.

Paste brush Choose a paste brush which is at least 100mm (4in) wide and keep it only for pasting.

Smoothing brush Also known as a paperhanger's brush, this has stiff bristles and is used to press a wallcovering into place. It should be kept very clean and dry.

Sponge This is useful for wiping up surplus paste while it is still wet.

Seam roller This small wood or plastic roller is used for pressing down seams once a covering is hung. Do not use it on embossed coverings as you will get 'tramlines'.

Plumb line and weight Used to produce true verticals in order to align paper, builders' line will hang better than string.

Steel tape

Sanding pad A sanding pad is useful for rubbing over stripped walls prior to papering.

Clean rag Choose a lint-free rag, such as old sheet, for wiping the pasting table as pasting progresses. Other rags may leave little fibres on the table.

Water trough For ready-pasted wallcoverings you will need a water-resistant trough in which to soak your cut piece of paper.

Paint roller With delicate wallcoverings, you may find a clean foam roller better than a brush for smoothing down. Apply a light pressure.

Steps You will need a pair of steps in order to reach the top of your wallcovering. (*See also opposite page, Safe Access.*)

*1. Bucket to hold paste, **2**. Retractable steel rule for measuring, **3**. Sponge for cleaning up, **4**. Wallpapering scissors, **5**. Craft knife, **6**. Pasting brush, **7**. Plumb line and bob for finding a true vertical, **8**. Chalk for string when snapping marker lines, **9**. Seam roller, **10**. Smoothing brush, **11**. Lining paper*

SAFE ACCESS

Safe access is vital, for many decorating accidents are due to carelessness about safety. Comfort is also important: standing on the rung of a ladder for hours on end can be hard on the instep, but working from a static platform surrounded by a safety rail is easy.

Steps

It is best to own at least one pair of steps – about five tread for inside and seven tread for outside work on a bungalow. For a house or upper floor flat you will also need an extending ladder. Any other necessary equipment can be hired for occasional use. (*See page 25, Hiring Equipment.*)

Personal safety

With all access equipment, it is wise to establish good working habits from the outset. Make sure ladders are firmly anchored and will not move when climbed. Never climb a ladder with your arms full – and hold on to the rungs, not the rails.

Never work too high up on a pair of steps. You should always have something to hold on to – ideally this should be the grab rail. If steps feel unsteady, re-site them and ask someone to hold on to the base.

LADDER SAFETY

To make ladder-work outside the house secure, screw galvanized ring bolts into the fascia board (the board to which gutters are fixed) at 1 metre (3ft) intervals.

When the ladder is erected, run cord through the nearest bolt and around a ladder rung, and tie it. As you move the ladder, tie it to the next nearest bolt.

Even with a secure ladder, never be tempted to lean from it. Climb down and re-site.

IMPROVISED PLATFORM

A platform can be safely made with a scaffold board and any secure stepladders with rungs at the same height. It is not usually necessary to buy a pair of identical stepladders.

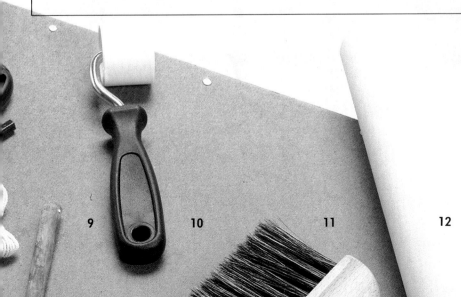

Improvised platform

Securing the top of a ladder

Staking the base of a ladder

To anchor the base of a ladder, tie ropes to a lower rung and to wooden stakes, driven into the ground. Anti-slip end caps are also available for ladder feet. Secure near a window by tying it to a strong, long wooden batten inside the frame.

9   10   11   12

Above: Dual-purpose ladders form steps or extend. Attachments include stabilizers, a foot rest, ladder tray and ladder stay.
Below: How the parts of a scaffold platform fit together

SCAFFOLD SAFETY

A static platform must have a firm, hard base upon which to stand. It should never be stood on garden soil, even on planks. It must not exceed 4.5 metres (15ft) in height if it is for static use, or 1.8 metres (6ft) if it is to be moved around on wheels. It is a good idea always to secure the tower to the house.

When erecting or climbing on to the tower, always climb up the inside. If you climb up the outside it is likely to tip with your weight.

Never attempt to move the tower if there are loose items lying on the working platform. Items falling from that height could cause a serious accident.

Inside Work

Steps Choose a pair with at least five steps, a platform and grab rail. Aluminium are much lighter than timber steps, but are not as stable.

Working platform For ceiling work there should be about 7cm (3in) between your head and the ceiling, in order to work comfortably. Make a platform from two pairs of steps or a pair of steps and a stout box with a scaffold board running between them – or simply hire trestles.

Staircase platform Designed to be used in confined spaces, you can hire a platform in sections for easy assembly. Alternatively, improvise with a ladder section against the wall, and steps (or a box) on the landing, with a board running between the ladder and steps.

Outside Work

Stepladder Choose a stepladder with at least seven steps, a platform and grab rail. An alternative, useful

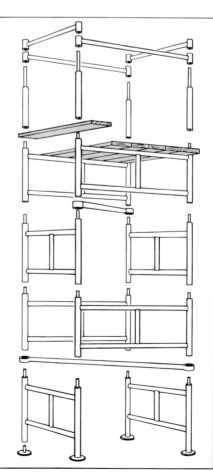

for a bungalow, would be a combination ladder which doubles as both steps and ladder.

Trestles Two decorating trestles, with a scaffold board running between them, give easy access to walls for repointing and so on. They can be hired.

Ladders These are made from wood or alloy. Timber is warmer to the touch in cold weather but heavy, and you must watch out for signs of deterioration. Alloy is much lighter and needs no protection, and is probably the best choice for DIY work.

Your ladder should extend at least three rungs above gutter level so that you always have something to hold on to. For most homes, a double-extension ladder will suffice.

A triple-extension ladder will have a higher reach, but it is quite difficult to handle and erect on your own. If you have to climb very high up, then cord control will help but it has to be built into the ladder: you can buy ladders with sash-cord running over pulleys to lift the ladder sections up by pulling the cord.

Ladder bracket Sometimes called a stand-off, this device slips over rungs near the top of the ladder to lift it away from the wall. It makes working near the top of the ladder easier and is useful for gutter work.

Ladder platform This simple, tray-like device hooks over a rung and rests on another to provide a safe platform on which to stand. When a lot of ladder work has to be done, a platform is much easier on the feet.

Ladder stays A number of devices are available to bolt or clamp to the base of a ladder to improve its stability and minimize movement.

Cripples Not much used in DIY work, a pair of them locked on to two ladders provides brackets upon which a scaffold board can be laid to give a working platform. Useful for wall work, they are best hired.

Platform tower This is the ideal working platform for decorating as it provides safe and comfortable access to walls. Supplied in sections, it is easily assembled on site. Wheels are provided for easy moving.

HIRING EQUIPMENT

Many decorating jobs can be made much easier with professional equipment. While it does not always make economic sense to buy professional equipment, especially for one-off jobs, it can be hired for a reasonable charge. An equipment hire catalogue will show you what is available when you have a particular project in mind.

Hire Charges

Hire charges are based on the length of time for which items are borrowed, so it pays to plan work carefully so that hired equipment is not left unused for days. There is an extra charge for delivery and collection of hire equipment. This may be necessary with large items.

Using Hire Equipment

If you have never used a type of equipment before, get as much advice as you can about how to use it – especially on any safety aspects. Some equipment can be dangerous if handled incorrectly.

Items can usually be booked in advance at no extra cost. When you collect hire equipment, be ready to give proof of your address and to pay a deposit. The hire charge is usually deducted from the deposit upon return of the item, and the balance refunded. You will be held responsible for looking after any equipment you borrow.

Protection

You may be advised with certain items to use protective clothing to protect your eyes, face and/or hands. Safety wear is not usually available for hire. *(See also page 26, Care and Protection.)*

BUYING AND HIRING

If you are planning large projects which will take time to complete or have to be spread over a long period, it may pay you to buy rather than hire. Equipment you might decide to buy includes a concrete mixer, platform tower, and extra extension ladders. If in good condition, could be re-sold after use.

If you are not sure whether to buy or hire, compare the prices in a hire catalogue with a current price guide. Hire catalogues list hire costs by hours, days and weeks for each item.

To help you transport items, you may also be able to loan free a roof rack or ladder rack.

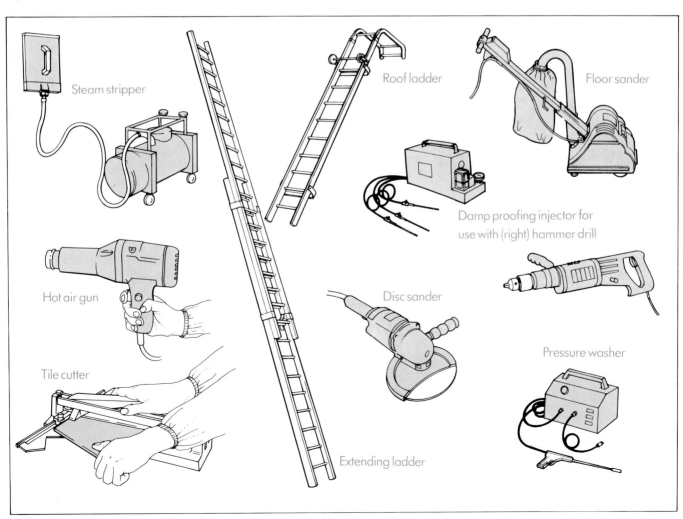

Steam stripper

Roof ladder

Floor sander

Damp proofing injector for use with (right) hammer drill

Hot air gun

Disc sander

Tile cutter

Pressure washer

Extending ladder

CARE AND PROTECTION

Many DIY jobs encountered around the home call for some form of protective clothing. You will have to use your common sense about when to wear protective clothing, and be guided by manufacturers' recommendations on products. Safety gear has become increasingly available, and is a necessary investment.

Face protection

Safety specs and goggles These lightweight eye protectors have polycarbonate lenses which are very tough. Never rely on normal glasses. Wear safety specs when tackling any job where pieces of material might fly, such as when you are wire-brushing metal or drilling masonry. Always wear them when using chemicals like paint stripper. Most specs and goggles are designed to fit over normal glasses.

Face mask A number of types are available, but all contain a simple filter to prevent dust particles entering the lungs via the nose and mouth. Wear one when doing any job which produces dust such as drilling, sanding old paintwork and laying glass fibre insulation. Remember the filter will not prevent you from inhaling fumes such as those from woodworm killer fluid – hire a respirator for that.

Damage from noise

Either ear plugs or ear protectors (DIY headphones) should be worn when you are using power tools in confined spaces – especially when using hammer action drills.

Skin protection

Gloves All kinds of hand protection are available, from simple disposable polythene gloves to heavy-duty leather gloves which protect hands from physical damage. Cotton gloves are ideal for normal work as they protect hands without making the skin sweat. Rubber and plastic can only be worn for short periods.

Coveralls Lightweight overalls in non-woven fabrics come in a range of sizes. Wear them for most dirty jobs from washing down to painting.

Protective clothing is essential. You will need safety specs for eyes, a mask to protect nose and lungs, ear muffs for noisy work, plus gloves and coveralls

Making light work

Tool belts These have been widely used by professionals for many years, but are now becoming popular for DIY jobs, as they enable you to keep your hands free of clutter. Belts can house both tools and accessories, and they are particularly recommended for ladder work, where you may want both hands free to hold on to the ladder.

Some building work calls for extra protection. A safety helmet and reinforced shoes or boots are a must.

EMERGENCY KIT

Spend time listing all likely emergencies which could crop up at home, then assemble a kit of items which could help you in emergencies. Pin a list of the items in the kit on the door of the cupboard where the kit is housed. Keep two of all disposables and, as soon as one is used, replace it. Include:

- First-aid kit for minor accidents
- Domestic fire extinguisher to relevant British Standards
- Glass fibre fire blanket for snuffing out cooker fires
- Torch (rechargeable, ideally)
- Replacement bulbs for all lights
- Spare fuses or fuse wire
- Electricians' screwdriver
- Insulated pliers
- Roll of insulating tape

PREPARATION

Ninety per cent of the battle in DIY is in the preparation of surfaces. It usually involves the most dirt and mess, yet the successful application of decorative materials depends on good preparation. Virtually all complaints about good quality decorative products can be traced back to surfaces unsuitable for the product.

Timetable

Make stage one a plan of campaign, known by the experts as a Critical Path Analysis. It merely means you have worked out a rough timetable of events, working in all the remedial jobs necessary. This is particularly important if you are involving tradesmen, perhaps to rewire, install central heating, replaster or treat for damp.

Wherever possible, strip the room if major work is being undertaken. Remove curtains and rails, carpets and underlays, wall lights and shelving. Then cover the floor with cotton dust sheets. Do not use polythene ones: they become slippery when wet and attract dust. At this stage, tackle alterations or additions – such as fitting a fireplace; installing new wiring, sockets or switches; repairs to joinery; installing coving; repairing plasterwork; fitting new windows; installing a fan in a kitchen or bathroom; making alterations to plumbing or central heating; dealing with damp or stains on ceilings – or anything else which would make a mess.

Materials

As you list jobs to be done, start to compile another list of all the materials you will need, with a rough guide to quantities. This is also the time to order any items you will need after preparation – some of which may need to be ordered well in advance to allow for delivery time. Use the following pages of tools and materials as a checklist.

PAPERING BEHIND FITTINGS

When you are wallpapering and fittings like curtain rails have been removed, you will need to mark the holes left by them. Before new wallcoverings go up, push a piece of matchstick in each hole. As the wallcovering is applied, push the matchsticks through the covering, leaving small, tell-tale holes.

---

1. Wire brush to remove crumbling material, 2. Stiff-bristled brush for use on flaking surfaces, 3 and 4. Two sizes of wallpaper and paint scraper, 5. Shaped shavehook for getting into mouldings, 6, 7 and 8. Grades of glasspaper, 9. Shaped skarsten scraper with a reversible blade, for removing paint, 10. Narrow scraper, 11. Sanding pad, 12 and 13. Shaped heads to direct flame, for 14. Blowtorch

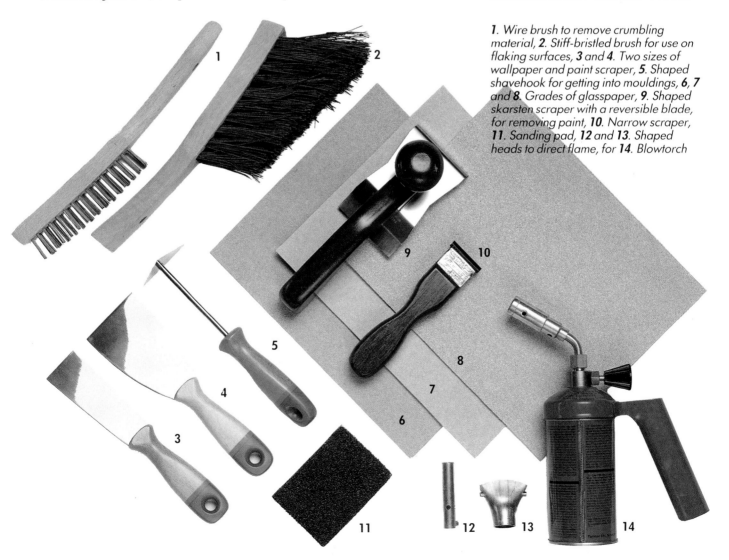

MATERIALS

It is important to choose the correct material for the job in hand, which is not always easy given the wide range of materials available. Before you buy, research what is available, and make sure that what you have in mind is compatible with the job in hand – and that nothing better has been introduced since you last decorated.

It is best to work with one brand of paint when buying primer, undercoat and top coat. The various paints will have been formulated to work well together. Remember that there are primers and finishes specially produced to suit particular surfaces, whether of rusted or galvanized metal, stained plaster or bare wood.

When choosing paints or papers, look for the batch number and check that it tallies with all the cans or rolls you buy. A different batch number could mean the paints or papers are slightly different in colour.

Remember your choice of materials may also be affected by whether you are working indoors or outdoors. Special paints, varnishes, sealants and fillers are available for external use.

PAINTS

Paints are available in a very wide range of colours – some ready-mixed and others produced in sophisticated mixing machines to order. Colour cards and match pots will help you make your choice.

Most paint shades are available in a high gloss, a silky sheen or matt finish. As a general rule, the higher the gloss, the easier the paint sheds dirt – though you may think that the sheens look more attractive. The traditional paint system consists of three materials as follows:

Primer This is used to seal the pores of a surface to stop the decorative coat sinking in. Primers are available for wood, metal and plaster, though there are also universal primers suitable for all three. In addition there are aluminium primers for tough conditions and quick-primers for rapid drying.
Undercoat This is specially formulated to obliterate the previous colour and give body to the new coating. Undercoat is incorporated with some gloss paints.
Top coat This is purely a protective coating, and is usually quite thin. It will not hide an under-colour unless it is a gloss paint with an undercoat incorporated. Otherwise you will need an undercoat for that purpose. You will find top coats available in gloss, silk and matt, and some have additives like polyurethane or polyester to make them tougher. The gloss may be a liquid, or it may have a jelly-like consistency.

Microporous paints

In addition to the traditional three-coat system are one- and two-coat systems for exterior painting. The paints used are microporous, designed to go straight on to bare wood with no primer or undercoat. Any moisture trapped under a microporous paint evaporates, as the paint skin 'breathes'.

With the one-coat system, a maximum of two coats can be applied. With the two-coat system, two special paints are used together. Although these paints can be used over old paint, they lose the microporous advantage which prevents blistering and flaking.

Emulsion paints

Emulsion paints are designed for large areas like walls and ceilings. Being water-based, they are not ideal for bare wood as they raise the grain as water soaks in. They are available in two main forms: as a thick liquid, and as a semi-solid in a tray. The emulsion in the tray can be lifted out on a paint roller. The act of rolling softens the paint enough to enable it to be spread easily. The main emulsion finishes are vinyl matt and vinyl silk.

Special paints and finishes

Special paints and finishes include enamels, varnishes and seals.
Enamel and lacquer paint This paint has been finely ground to give a very high gloss finish. No primer or undercoat is needed in conjunction with it on wood or metal, and it

It is important to use only lead-free paint when decorating children's rooms, furniture or toys

is quite safe to use in a nursery.
Rust-resisting finishes These consist of enamel formulated to inhibit rust. No primer or undercoat is required, and they are available in a smooth or hammered (indented) finish.
Radiator enamel Specially formulated to hold a pure white tone even under high temperatures.
Anti-condensation paint This emulsion contains additives to bulk it out and form an insulative layer on walls or ceilings. It also contains fungicide to help prevent mould.
Tile red paint Used for brightening jaded brick or coating tiled sills, this paint is for interior or exterior use.
Special metal paint Designed to adhere firmly to galvanized metal and aluminium – two surfaces which have always been difficult to paint. It requires no primer or undercoat.

Neutralize rust by using a primer which reacts with rust and forms a barrier between the metal and air and moisture

Heat-resisting paint Metallic paints are available only in a limited colour range. They will resist heat up to 250°C (500°F). No primer is required.

Floor and cork seal Based on polyurethane, this paint forms a tough, non-slip coating on wood and cork. It provides an alternative to floor varnish.

Floor paint Used widely industrially, floor paint forms a very tough

The way a front door is decorated sets the scene for any visitor to your home. Stain and varnish or paint are equally effective

---

CALCULATING PAINT QUANTITIES

Calculating just how much paint you need for a given area is not easy. For apart from the area involved, the porosity of the material being painted and its texture will affect the quantity you need.

For smooth, sealed surfaces, be guided by the coverage listed on the can, but for a pebbledashed exterior wall you can double the amount needed for an equivalent smooth area. As a general guide 1 litre covers as follows:

General purpose primer 10-12 sq m (11-13 sq yd)
Undercoat 16 sq m (18 sq yd)
Gloss paint 15 sq m (17-17 sq yd)
One-coat gloss 10 sq m (11 sq yd)
Emulsion paint 10-14 sq m (11-15 sq yd)
Masonry paint 4-10 sq m (4-11 sq yd), according to surface

To calculate for any given room, make a simple drawing, and divide the walls into easily-calculated areas – above the door, below the window, and so on. Multiply the width by the height of each area and add them all together.

For standard windows with a number of glazing bars, multiply the width of the window by the depth and calculate as for a solid area. For large picture windows deduct 50 per cent. For metal windows deduct 25 per cent.

For flush doors merely multiply the height of the doors by the width and add another 10 per cent for edges. For a panelled door add 25 per cent. A little extra paint stored in a marked jar is always useful for touching-up. *(See page 50, Storing Paint.)*

---

decorative surface on concrete, stone, brick or wood. It is abrasion-resistant, making it ideal for a garage or workshop floor, and can provide a temporary floor treatment within the home.

Textured coatings These special compounds are applied thickly to walls or ceilings to produce a textured decorative finish. They are ideal for covering blemishes.

Roofing paint Mainly based on bitumen and rubber, roofing paint is thickly applied to provide a tough, weatherproof skin. It is mainly used on flat roofs.

Masonry paints Many exterior masonry paints contain additives such as sand, mica or nylon fibre. This adds texture, seals fine cracks and toughens the paint.

Varnishes Great strides have been made in varnish production, and a wide range is available for both indoor and outdoor use. Varnishes may be colourless or have stains added. Some are microporous, have ultra-violet filters to protect against the sun's rays and contain fungicides to discourage mould.

There is a wide range of stain and varnish colours. Here are some of them. From top to bottom: ebony wood dye, mahogany wood dye, blueberry clear satin varnish, fir green woodstain, oak polyurethane gloss, pine polyurethane gloss, and clear satin polyurethane varnish

Aerosols

Paint in aerosol cans is ideal for small touch-up jobs, stencilling, and for tackling awkward surfaces such as cane, wicker or wrought iron. Do not paint very large areas requiring a number of cans.

Remember that paint from an aerosol is very thin, as it has to come out of a fine nozzle. Shake it well before use, then hold it at the distance recommended on the can and spray with an action parallel with the work – never in an arc. (See page 21, Spray Guns.)

Apply only a very thin coat, or it will run. Then build up, coat upon coat, until you have the required density of colour.

Preservative finishes

Most timbers need some form of preservative treatment when used out of doors. The exception is pre-treated timber – which you may recognize by the greenish tinge to the wood. It has been factory-impregnated. Another exception is Western red cedar, which contains natural preservative oils. Unfortunately the rich red colour bleaches out to a dull grey with weathering. There are, however, preservatives with a stain designed for cedar which artificially bring back the colour of the wood.

Preservatives used to contain solvents, such as creosote, most of which were harmful to plant life. However, today's water-based preservatives have no unpleasant smell and are harmless to plants.

Most coloured preservatives are based upon natural wood tones. They may be used either for refreshing a wood colour, or for completely transforming the colour. For example, jaded light oak could be enlivened with a warm mahogany colour. A clear preservative is also available for treating wood which is later to be painted.

A range of decorative oil-stain preservatives is available which are a cross between a paint and a preservative. They give a highly decorative finish to timber, while preserving it and inhibiting mould growth. Most oil-stains come in wood tones, though some are coloured, and give a slightly translucent sheen allowing the natural wood grain to show through. Many are also microporous, so that any moisture trapped in the wood can evaporate.

Outside, items which will be subjected to heavy weathering, such as wooden fence posts, will need more than a superficial coating of preservative to protect them. It is a good idea to make a trough from heavy-gauge polythene, fill it with preservative and submerge the posts in the preservative. Weight them down and leave to soak.

Left: Aerosol sprays are ideal for use with stencils. Pick those which are ozone friendly and use a number of light sprays. One thick coat will run

Below: Preservative finishes come in a range of wood stains and other colours. Pre-treated, factory-impregnated timber is also available

WALLCOVERINGS

The term 'wallpaper' is much mis-used, for while wallcoverings have paper backings, they may be faced with a number of different materials. However, as it is convenient to refer to an abbreviated term, 'paper' is used here as a generic term for all types of wallcovering.

A standard roll is 10 metres × 530mm (33ft × 21in). The paper comes ready-trimmed and is usually polythene-wrapped to keep it clean.

The chart for calculating wall-paper quantities is based on the standard roll size. (*See page 34.*) Many continental papers, however, do not conform to this size, so when selecting from continental books, look in the front of the pattern book for roll sizes and a guide to coverage.

Each roll of paper will be stamped with a production number. When selecting rolls, check that all the production numbers are the same. If not, there may be slight variations in colour and shading as the paper has been produced in a different batch run. For this reason, it is always wise to over-order rather than under-order, for ordering one or two rolls at a later date often means you will be supplied from a different batch. If you do order too many rolls, usually you will be allowed to return any which are unused and still sealed in their polythene wraps.

Another variable on wallcoverings is the pattern repeat. The bigger the repeat, the more likely it is that extra rolls will be required due to wastage of paper between lengths. For economy, choose a close repeat. Or, to make decorating easier, look for papers with a random repeat which do not need any matching. (*See also pages 8-13, Colour, Pattern and Texture.*)

Some materials have nothing to match – such as hessians or silks. You will have to accept, however, that seams on plain wallcoverings will be more noticeable than with

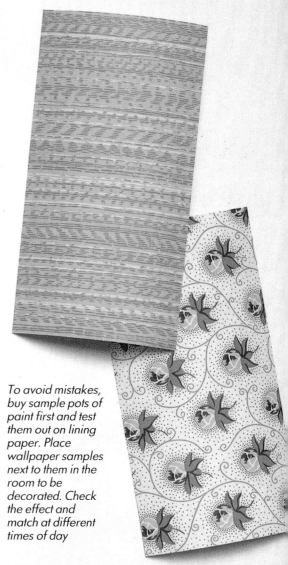

To avoid mistakes, buy sample pots of paint first and test them out on lining paper. Place wallpaper samples next to them in the room to be decorated. Check the effect and match at different times of day

matching patterns. (*See also page 63, Hanging Special Wallcoverings.*)

Easy-strip coverings, as the name implies, can readily be removed from the wall when you wish to redecorate. The surface covering can be peeled away from the backing without soaking. If it is smoothly applied to the wall, the backing paper may be left in place or, if you wish to remove it, a light soaking will suffice.

Ready-pasted coverings come coated with sufficient paste to hang the materials. You activate the paste by dipping the length of paper in water just prior to hanging it. When papering sealed wall surfaces like painted walls, you may find there is too much paste, as none can soak through the paint into the plaster. If so, simply wipe away any surplus paste.

DAMP PREVENTION

Many outside walls – particularly those which are north facing – tend to be cold to the touch. This encourages condensation which causes damp patches and the growth of discolouring moulds. Cavity walls can be insulated professionally, and this should solve the problem. It helps to line walls that are solid with sheet expanded polystyrene before papering. Use a tough wallcovering over the top, as the insulation is easily dented.

The main wallcoverings you are likely to come across are as follows:

Lining paper A smooth, unpatterned paper which is designed to cover poor wall and ceiling surfaces prior to the use of a decorative material. It is not often used as there are textured wallcoverings, both decorative and plain for painting, which will disguise poor walls without the use of lining paper.

Standard wallpaper This is a single sheet of paper in different weights, on which a pattern is printed.

Duplex wallpaper Consisting of two sheets of paper bonded together, this is less likely to tear than standard paper. The decorative paper is often textured.

Smooth vinyl This decorative sheet of PVC is bonded to a paper backing. Modern printing techniques make it hard to distinguish some vinyls from paper. The surface is tough and easy-to-clean.

Embossed vinyl Sheet PVC is moulded to give a high relief pattern. This is then mounted on a tough paper backing to produce the embossed type of vinyl.

Blown vinyl Here a coating of vinyl is expanded during manufacture to produce a relief pattern. It has a smooth paper backing.

Novamura An unusual foamed plastic material which feels like thin fabric, Novamura is pressed on to adhesive which has already been applied to the wall. It is easy to hang.

Relief wallcoverings These are heavy papers which are embossed with a pattern during manufacture. Unlike vinyl wallcoverings, the paper is not backed. More paste is therefore required, as hollows in the emboss fill up. Care must be taken not to press out the emboss when you are smoothing the paper on the wall. Heavier relief papers are known as Lincrustas, made of putty-like materials from which the pattern is moulded. *(See also pages 58–68, Using Wallcoverings.)*

GOOD SEAMS

Some of the heavy special wallcoverings may not meet well at the seams. The secret is to overlap adjoining pieces as you hang them, then use a sharp craft knife and steel straight-edge to cut through both layers. Remove the two waste strips and you will have a perfect matching join.

Cork tiling and low lighting lend warmth to this bathroom

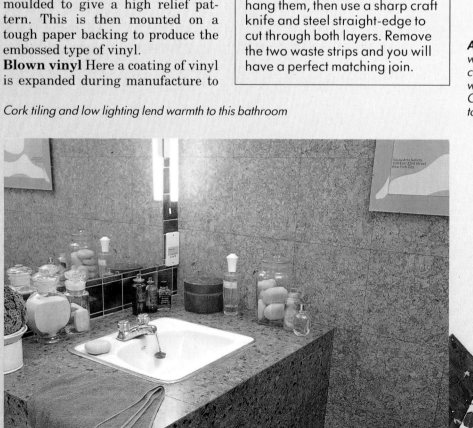

Above: *Hessian wallcoverings come in various weaves.* **Below:** *Cork is bonded on to a painted* *backing that can be seen behind the cork, creating a pattern. Woven cane makes an effective covering for cupboard doors*

You can match some watered silk blinds or curtains with special silk wallcoverings

Metallic As the name implies, the covering consists of a thin metal foil bonded to a paper backing. Modern machinery has made possible some vivid effects. Paste metallics in the same way as wallpaper.

Flock Hanging a flock used to be one of the most difficult wallpapering operations, until the advent of nylon fibres. Today's flocks made with nylon fibres have the ability to recover when flattened and are far easier to handle. Surplus paste can be wiped away without marking the flock. Paste them in the same way as wallpaper.

Grasscloth For this material, real grasses are bonded to a fine paper backing, then thread is woven through to hold the materials together. Paste the wall, and apply the covering to it.

Special Wallcoverings

Special effects can be created by using natural materials like cork and silk, and by means of clever reproduction processes which give very realistic imitations of materials like timber panelling and tiling. In the main they are used as features in a room rather than for overall decoration.

Cost may also regulate their use. Most of these materials are expensive, so it is essential that the walls to which they are hung are well prepared. Walls must be clean and dry. Also it is wise to use pastes containing a fungicide to reduce the risk of mould growth. *(See also page 63, Hanging Special Wallcoverings.)*

Far right: Fabric wallcoverings come in as varied materials as wool and silk. Used effectively, a silk wallcovering will look luxurious, while mixed woollen thread will lend warmth. Hang them in areas where there is little likelihood of damage

Relief papers Designed to be painted, these are available in a number of effects, including brick wall, stone wall, timber panelling and plaster daub.

Relief vinyls Many of these are cushioned and give remarkably realistic photo-reproductions of decorative materials like timber panelling and ceramic wall tiling. They provide an economic alternative to the real thing.

Hessian The easiest to use is hessian bonded to a tough paper backing, as the backing helps retain the shape of the material. Hessian is available in a number of colours, and is pasted in the same way as heavy wallpaper. *(See also page 63, Hanging Special Wallcoverings.)*

Cork Here, very thin veneers of cork are bonded to a plain or painted backing paper so that a colour shows through the holes in the cork. Paste is applied to the wall rather than to the paper.

Silk Here, the delicate fabric is bonded to a paper backing to make it easy to hang. A material like this is best used in protected areas like alcoves where there is little chance of scuffing. It is pasted in the same way as a heavy paper.

FINISHED EFFECTS

When choosing special coverings, bear in mind there are also covings, ceiling centres and imitations, beams and corbels which you can use to complement the chosen covering.

If you have traditional fibrous plasterwork (such as plaster mouldings and cornices) and wish to renew or extend it, some specialist companies produce it using original moulds. Beams are available in natural wood or moulded in foam plastics.

CALCULATING WALLPAPER QUANTITIES

Working out the number of rolls of wallcovering required for any room is not an exact science. The amount is affected by a number of factors: the height to be papered is relevant, for how the height measurement divides into a roll length determines how much wastage there will be.

The pattern repeat must also be taken into account. With a random pattern needing no matching, there is no wastage between lengths. With a large pattern repeat, you may find that you have to cut away a large amount of paper in order to make the pattern fit, therefore you will get fewer complete lengths from a roll. Sometimes you can compensate for this by cutting lengths from alternate rolls of paper and trying the pattern against the length just hung. It is wise to buy one or two extra rolls – often these can be returned unopened if not required.

Note the size of the pattern repeat of your chosen paper from the wrapping. Check whether it is of standard width and length – 10 metres × 530mm (33ft × 21in). The chart on this page is for standard size rolls of wallcovering. If you have chosen from a continental range, look at the information and estimating chart for that range.

The batch number of each roll should match or the colours may vary slightly. If for any reason you have to accept a roll or two from a different batch, plan to use them in areas where they will not be immediately obvious – behind a wardrobe or in alcoves, for example.

For walls

The estimating chart will help you calculate the amount of paper required, or make your own calculations. You must work throughout in either metric or imperial, but not both. Proceed as follows: measure the distance from the skirting board to picture rail or ceiling, depending on how far up you are papering. Then measure the total distance around the room, taking into account in your calculations doors and standard (but not picture) windows. If you have picture windows, you can deduct their area from your calculations.

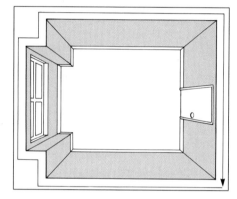

Measure the circumference as indicated

Multiply the distance around the walls by the height to find the total wall area to be covered. Now multiply the width of your chosen wallcovering by the total length of a roll to find out the area of each roll. Divide the wall area by the roll area and the resulting figure is the approximate number of rolls required. However, do not forget to order extra rolls if you have a large pattern repeat.

Ceilings

Simply divide the area of the ceiling by the area of a roll for the number of rolls required.

Calculating number of rolls for walls

Height from skirting	8.53m (27ft 9in)	9.75m (31ft 8in)	10.97m (35ft 8in)	12.19m (39ft 7in)	13.41m (43ft 7in)	14.63m (47ft 7in)	15.83m (51ft 5in)	17.07m (55ft 6in)	18.29m (59ft 5in)	19.51m (63ft 5in)	20.73m (67ft 4in)	21.95m (71ft 4in)	23.16m (75ft 3in)
2.13-2.29m (7ft-7ft 6in)	4	4	5	5	6	6	7	7	8	8	9	9	9
2.30-2.44m (7ft 6in-8ft)	4	4	5	5	6	6	7	8	8	9	9	10	10
2.45-2.59m (8ft-8ft 6in)	4	5	5	6	6	7	7	8	8	9	9	10	10
2.60-2.74m (8ft 6in-9ft)	4	5	5	6	6	7	8	8	9	9	10	11	11
2.75-2.90m (9ft-9ft 6in)	4	5	6	6	7	7	8	9	9	10	10	11	12
2.91-3.05m (9ft 6in-10ft)	5	5	6	7	7	8	9	9	10	10	11	12	12
3.06-3.20m (10ft-10ft 6in)	5	5	6	7	8	8	9	10	10	11	12	12	13

Calculating number of rolls for a ceiling

Measurement around room	9.75m (32ft)	10m (32ft 10in)	11m (36ft)	11.5m (37ft 9in)	12m (39ft 4in)	12.8m (42ft)	13.4m (44ft)	14m (46ft)	14.5m (47ft 6in)	15.8m (51ft 10in)
Number of rolls required	2	2	2	2	2	3	3	3	3	4
Measurement around room	16.5m (54ft 2in)	17m (55ft 10in)	17.5m (57ft 5in)	18m (59ft)	19m (62ft 4in)	19.5m (64ft)	20m (65ft 8in)	20.5m (67ft 3in)	21m (69ft)	22.5m (73ft 10in)
Number of rolls required	4	4	4	5	5	5	5	6	6	7

WALL TILES

Tiling has a number of advantages as a means of wall decoration. Tiles come in an attractive range of patterns, they can be wiped clean and are long-lasting. Tiling is also a very pleasant means of decorating, whereby you are working with small, manageable units which are easily applied. You can also cover as much or as little of the wall area in one session as you wish.

Decorative effects

Since tiles offer a permanent form of decoration, it is wise to spend time planning where to use them and what effect you want to achieve. You could buy them in a colour which blends with your kitchen units or bathroom suite. Patterned tiles should complement the function or atmosphere of the room. You may wish to intersperse patterned tiles with plain, or to have groups of pictorial tiles. Do you prefer a matt finish or a high gloss?

Consider, too, tile size and shape. Standard tiles are easy to obtain. Unusual tiles or non-standard-sized tiles generally have to be ordered. The actual form of tiles has changed: on most tiles there are no longer any spacing nibs. (*See page 94, Glossary.*) To get your spacing correct, packets of plastic cross-shaped spacers are available to fit in the corners of each tile. These are very cheap, and are left in place and grouted over.

Tiles tend to be supplied in packs of mixed edges. Packs contain tiles for both main body tiling and finished edge tiles. Standard packs of tiles cover a specific area. Matching decorative tiles are sold either singly or in packs. Make a rough plan of where to place them before you buy.

Planning your design

If you wish to intersperse decorative tiles with plain tiles it is sometimes difficult to know exactly where to place them for best effect. To get a feel for the right balance of patterned and plain tiles, cut out squares of tile-sized paper and fix them to the walls with Blu-tack, moving them around until you are happy with the arrangement. Lay out bought tiles over a large, flat surface area and juggle them around until you achieve a pleasing design. Keep feature tiles at least one tile out from room corners or the eye will be led to wall edges rather than to the central areas of pattern.

Boxed sets of tiles which produce a small mural are also available and can be used to provide an attractive focal point in an area of plain tiling. When estimating quantities remember to allow for any feature tiles.

Above: Here white tiles with a tiny motif highlight the smart striped wallpaper
Right: Ceramic wall tiles come in a huge range of colours, designs, textures and shapes. Border and edging tiles are available that provide a neat finish when walls are half-tiled only. Plain tiles can be interspersed with patterned ones, but lay the tiles out on the floor first to get the spacing right. Murals made up from a group of tiles are highly decorative

Cutting Tiles

Another factor which may influence your choice of tiles is their hardness. In the early days of tiling the backing of a tile, or the 'biscuit', was relatively soft, making tiles very easy to cut. Now a much tougher material is used. Tiles – especially imported ones – may be so hard that the old technique of scoring, and then snapping them over two matchsticks lined up with the score mark, just does not work. In this case, you need to invest in a semi-professional platform cutter with a sliding arm and inbuilt tile-snapper. Before ordering a large number of tiles, it will pay to buy a few first, to make sure you can cut them. If necessary, invest in a new tile cutter. You will also find a tile saw useful for shaping tiles to fit around obstructions.

Where tiles are vulnerable to knocks – such as on sills or the edges of worktops, there are matching plastic edging strips available which are laid under the edge row of tiles. For finishing off edges in contact with baths or basins, sets of ceramic quadrant (quarter-circle) mouldings can be obtained in matching colours.

For tiling you will need tile adhesive, to fix tiles in place, and tile grout, for sealing the gaps between

Plastic edging strip provides a durable edge where tiles are vulnerable, such as on worktop edges. It comes in a range of colours to co-ordinate with the room scheme

tiles. These are also available as a combined adhesive and grout. The disadvantage of the latter is that it is not easy to remove when dry, so any surplus on the tile surface must be removed immediately while still wet. Standard grout can be left as long as you wish and removed after hardening.

In areas which are likely to get damp, use water-resistant adhesive and grout. Special heat-resistant adhesives are available for areas

Use floor tiles for worktops – wall tiles are not tough enough – and waterproof grout

near heat such as fire surrounds.

Mosaic tiles are an attractive alternative. They come in sheets of small squares which are held together by a netting backing. The backing stays in place as you lay the sheets of tiles on a bed of adhesive. Then you fill the gaps between the mosaic pieces with grout, as for normal tiling.

CALCULATING TILE QUANTITIES

Boxes of tiles usually state the area the contents will cover, which makes calculating easier. To find out how many boxes of tiles you will need for a floor, simply measure the length and width of the room at the *widest* points, taking measurements in alcoves and into doorways to butt up to other floorings. Multiply the length by the width to find the room area, and divide this area by the area of the box contents. Work throughout in either imperial or metric but not both. To calculate the exact number of *tiles*, divide the room area by the area of one tile.

For wall tiles, calculate the wall area by multiplying the height by the width and divide this figure by the area of the box contents (or area of a tile).

Add an extra 5 per cent on to your total to allow for cut tiles and breakages.

With tile patterns, you will need to draw the dimensions of your room to scale on graph paper, and colour in your floor or wall design. Work out from this how many tiles in each colour or pattern you will need.

FLOOR TILES

The term 'tile' for flooring covers a variety of materials. In an awkwardly-shaped room with obstructions, easy-to-handle tiles are an attractive option. Laying a sheet floorcovering in such a room could be tricky. Types of tile include the following:

Vinyl Tough, wipe-clean vinyl tiles are available in a variety of patterns and finishes. Some have a self-adhesive backing, others are stuck down with special flooring adhesive.
Cork Cork makes for a comfortable and attractive covering in a kitchen, bathroom or breakfast room. Tiles are available ready-coated with polyurethane sealant. If you lay un-coated tiles, they should be sealed as soon as possible.
Carpet Ideal for small rooms and irregular areas, carpet tiles are easy to cut and lay. Some are held in place with double-sided tape, others are for loose-laying. An advantage of the carpet tile is that damaged or worn tiles can be swapped with better tiles from a less obtrusive area of the room, or replaced.
Parquet These hardwood squares, made up of individual fingers of wood arranged in a pattern, make an attractive, durable floorcovering. The tiles are stuck in place with special bitumen-based adhesive. Most come ready-sealed.
Ceramic Extra-thick ceramic tiles are available for flooring. They are best laid on concrete floors – as opposed to flexible timber floors – where there is no likelihood of movement. A special, heavy-duty tile cutter is advisable for cutting them.

CEILING TILES

The most common ceiling tile for domestic use is expanded polystyrene. Polystyrene tiles are easy to put up, come in a variety of sizes and patterns, and can be emulsioned.

All modern expanded polystyrene ceiling tiles self-extinguish if they contact fire, and must be stuck to a combed layer of adhesive.

Ceramic floor tiles come in a wide range of shapes, sizes and colours. Some are glazed, others have a textured or slip-resistant finish and are ideal for kitchens and bathrooms where spilt water can be dangerous. Some have the corners cut out and small square tiles in a second colour fit in to create the pattern. Ceramic tiles are best laid on solid floors.

When sticking polystyrene ceiling tiles in place with adhesive, right, stand on a scaffold platform. For maximum comfort, the top of your head should be about 7cm (3 in) from the ceiling

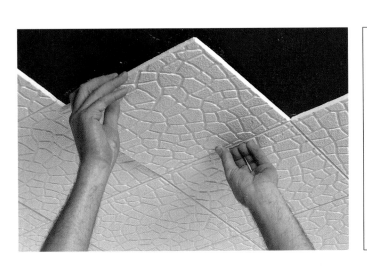

PAINTING CEILING TILES

It is easiest to coat expanded polystyrene ceiling tiles with emulsion paint *before* putting them up. Never use oil-based paints, which are a fire risk. Special fire-retardant paints are available for extra safety.

Stick ceiling tiles in place with the correct adhesive in order to minimize inflammability. Do not use contact adhesives: they melt tiles.

DECORATING SUNDRIES

Materials often vary according to whether they are for indoor or outdoor use. Make sure you have the right materials for the job in hand, using the following as a guide:

Cleaners The most common cause of bad paintwork is a dirty or greasy surface. Use domestic cleaning powders for general preparatory cleaning or sugar soap on particularly dirty surfaces. A strong solution of sugar soap will break down a high glaze on paint, making it better able to take a new coat. Liquid sander is a stronger still abrasive. You should always wash surfaces thoroughly after breaking down.

Fillers Cellulose-based fillers are used for small repairs to walls. Otherwise use acrylic sealant for areas where vibration may dislodge filler, such as around doors; silicone rubber for sealing gaps around basins, sinks and baths; an epoxy-based paste for repairs to wood or metal which is to be painted; plastic wood or special epoxy filler for cracks in timber if the surface is to be natural-finished.

For plaster repair, special one-coat repair plasters are available to fill holes up to 5cm (2in) deep. Plaster skim is for a final coat of plaster, and smooths over minor faults in a plastered wall or ceiling.

Putties Traditional linseed oil putty is for use around timber frames when glazing. Metal casement putty is designed for metal frames. Dual-purpose putty can be used on either metal or timber frames.

Acrylic glazing sealant is applied in a similar fashion to linseed oil putty. It does not dry out and crack as linseed oil putty does, but remains semi-flexible.

Adhesives Wallcovering adhesives are available both in powder form, for mixing with water, and ready-mixed in tubs. Use the adhesive recommended for your wallcovering. Some for vinyl contain fungicide to discourage mould.

Size is a weakened adhesive designed to prepare a dry wall surface and to add 'slip' so that a covering will slide easily into place.

Seam repair adhesive is for sticking down any vinyl wallcovering seams which may have lifted.

Fungicides Bleach can be used to deter mould, but has a limited effect. It is better to use a proprietary fungicide. Some outdoor decorative materials contain a fungicide.

PREPARATION

Assuming that all structural work has been carried out and the room has, as far as possible, been cleared, cover the bare floor with dust sheets. Use cotton, rather than plastic, ones. Polythene becomes slippery when wet and tends to attract dust which is then hard to remove. Group any remaining furniture in the centre of the room and cover it with a large dust sheet.

The order of work is important. It is always best to start with the ceiling (whether you paint or paper it) — even before stripping paper from walls. If walls are to be painted, emulsion them before any woodwork is given its final coat of paint. If they are to be papered, finish painting all the woodwork first, allowing the paint just on to the walls. Then if the wallcovering does not exactly butt up to the woodwork, the gap will be less obvious.

WALLS & CEILINGS

Walls

After the walls have been stripped (*see page 42, Stripping*), examine them for cracks and gaps in the plaster. Fill small cracks with a cellulose filler, working it into the cracks with a flexible filling knife and leaving it just proud of the wall surface. When set, smooth the filler down with a medium-grade glass-paper slotted onto a sanding block.

Large cracks With larger cracks, dig out all loose and crumbling material. Damp the hole and fill with plaster repair filler. Take the filler just proud of the wall surface and sand it level when set.

Cracks around the door and window frames should be cleared of loose material using the tip of a small trowel. Fill them with an acrylic sealant, which grips better than cellulose filler. Use the same material to fill any gaps along skirting boards.

Weak spots Cracks between walls and ceiling rarely stay sealed, whatever material you use. This is a weak area where any slight movement of a flat or house will re-open the cracks. It is better to use coving to hide a gap (*see page 41, All About Coving*) or, alternatively, lap ceiling paper down onto the walls to cover it.

A smooth surface If your walls are painted, wash them down with a strong solution of sugar soap to break any glaze on the surface. When all remedial work is done, rub over the walls with a flexible sanding pad and dust them off.

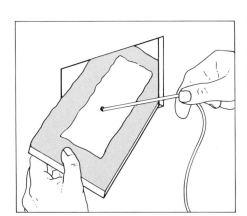

1 To patch plasterboard cut a piece slightly larger than the hole. Tie a nail to string and feed the string through a central hole. Dab the front edges of the board with plaster.

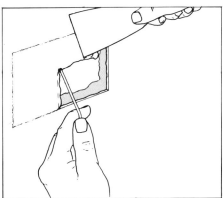

2 Place the board in the hole, plaster side facing you, pull the string tight and hold it while you add more plaster to almost fill the hole. Leave to set, cut the string and finish filling.

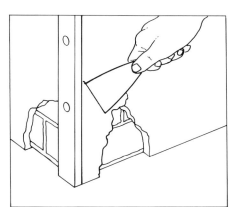

Damaged corner plaster can be repaired by pinning a batten to one side flush with corner. Fill the opposite side. When dry remove the batten, and repeat on opposite edge.

Ceilings

Once the ceiling has been stripped (*see page 42, Stripping*), check it for minor cracks. Fill them with cellulose filler as for walls. Occasionally a large crack runs right across a ceiling, opening and shutting with the seasons through slight movement of the house. This type of crack is virtually impossible to seal and is best disguised with, for example, ceiling tiles.

Stains Stains on a ceiling will sometimes bleed through new decoration if they are not treated. Seal the stained area either with aluminium prime-sealer, or with a proprietary stain block. A quick-drying one is available in aerosol form.

Steam stripper Old textured surfaces need only be washed down if they are to be repainted. If you wish to remove them, however, use either a steam wallpaper stripper to soften the compound, or one of the special stripping compounds available. Textured surfaces are difficult and messy to remove.

Doors

Panelled doors may show cracks where the wood has shrunk slightly. Fill them with an epoxy-based wood filler if the door is to be painted, or use a matching wood filler if the door is to be given a natural finish.

This will absorb a stain. When a filler has hardened, always rub it down with fine glasspaper, working *with* the wood grain in order to avoid scratches across the grain.

Gloss paint on doors needs flatting down with a strong solution of sugar soap, with liquid sander or with a damp flexible sanding pad. Wash well before repainting.

Windows

Smooth down any rough spots of paintwork, then wash the windows down with sugar soap. Kill off any

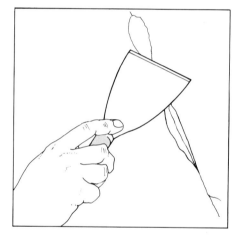

1 Use a filling knife to widen crack sides; remove loose debris. Damp the crevice then fill it just proud of the ceiling surface. Sand when dry.

areas of mould with a fungicide. More than one application may be needed in extreme cases.

Check old metal frames for signs of rust and remove any loose scale. Treat them with a rust inhibitor or metal priming paint. Repair any holes with an epoxy-based repair paste.

Frames, rails and skirtings

Fill holes and cracks with wood filler, then smooth down with fine glasspaper or use a damp, flexible sanding pad.

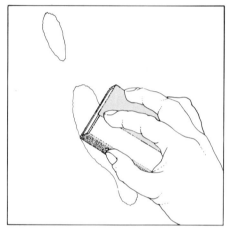

2 A deep crack may need a second application of filler. When dry, sand the surface flush with the surrounding ceiling plaster.

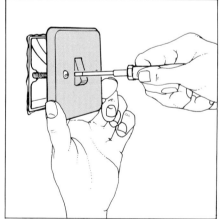

Cover light fittings, with power off, before decorating. Encase flex and fitting in a plastic bag held in place with adhesive tape.

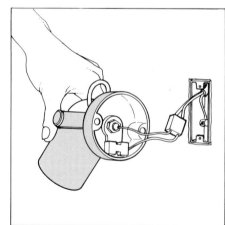

Partially unscrew light switches to make it easier to paint or paper around them. Do not tuck a foil wallcovering inside but trim around switch.

Disconnect wall lights putting them out of the way as you work. Always turn off electricity when working near exposed wires.

ALL ABOUT COVING

Coving provides a decoratiave divide between the walls and ceiling and will hide cracks

Coving is an attractive decorative feature, and also hides unsightly cracks which are often impossible to fill. Some coving may be painted before it is put up, so there is no risk of a contrasting paint colour running on to walls or ceiling, and it gives a highly finished effect. Put up new plaster coving before you paint or paper the ceiling and walls.

If you live in an older home you may have fibrous plaster coving in ornate designs. This is certainly worth preserving, and there are specialist companies still making coving to the original moulds. If you have damaged areas to repair, or wish to extend existing coving, you will probably find such a company listed in your local Yellow Pages under Plastering and Screeding.

New Coving

Expanded polystyrene This is available plain or patterned, mostly in 1 metre (yd) lengths about 100mm (4in) wide. Internal and external corner pieces are supplied with many types, so there is no complicated joining. Expanded polystyrene is light, fixing is by special adhesive. There is also a plaster-coated variety available.

Plaster Lengths of gypsum plaster coving encased in a tough paper are available either 100mm (4in) or 127mm (5in) wide and 2 metres (6½ft) long, although longer lengths are often available to order. Fixing is by special adhesive which must adhere to plain wall or ceiling plaster. You may find cutting mitres a little tricky but a template is supplied. Practise before you start.

You can now buy rolls of decorative strip for adding pattern and colour to plain plaster coving.

To add elegance to a ceiling, fit a ceiling centre. These are produced in polystyrene and in fibrous plaster to match older covings. The latter are supplied by the specialist companies referred to earlier.

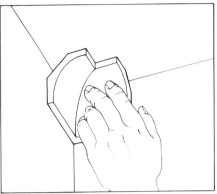

1 Start fixing polystyrene coving by fitting the corner pieces. Spread adhesive on the angled backs and push gently but firmly in place so that each corner fits snugly.

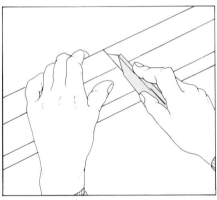

2 Measure the space between corner pieces and cut a length to fill the space. Use a trimming knife to cut.

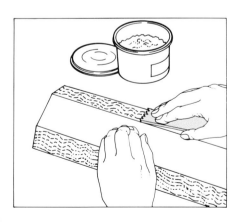

3 Smear adhesive on each reverse side of the coving length, then gently press and smooth the length in place. Use a damp rag to remove excess adhesive before it dries.

STRIPPING

With paintwork, the general rule for stripping is, if it is in good condition, do not remove it. However, if there are so many coats of paint that it is causing windows and doors to stick, or if it has been badly applied, then paint should be stripped.

With wallcoverings, the general rule is to remove them, unless they are of a type designed to be emulsion coated. Sometimes it is possible to paint over decorative wallcoverings, but it is wise to experiment first to see if the paper is affected by the water in the paint.

Wallcoverings

If a wallcovering needs soaking to remove it, the job can be made easier by using a steam wallpaper stripper. Domestic models are available at a reasonable price, otherwise the tool can be hired. Follow the precautions outlined under Ceiling Coverings.

Standard wallpaper To remove most wallpaper, use a steam stripper or soak the paper with a mixture of warm water, liquid detergent and a little wallpaper paste. The paste holds the water on the paper. Leave soaking for 20-30 minutes then lift it away with a flexible scraper.

Duplex paper Remove Duplex as for standard paper, but allow a longer soaking time.

Heavy papers Heavy embossed papers in particular will be firmly stuck in place. Roughing the surface with a coarse abrasive will help steam or water get into the paper. Allow plenty of soaking time.

Painted paper Break down the surface of the paper with a coarse abrasive pad soaked in water. (It is best not to use a wire brush, as small pieces of metal can get embedded in the wall plaster, leading to rust spots.) Soak and then strip.

Easy strip This wallcovering can be stripped by pulling the decorative layer away from the backing. You can also soak off the backing or leave it in place and paper over it. The surface is not suitable as a base for painting.

Vinyls Standard and blown vinyls have a backing and can be treated in the same way as easy-strips.

Hessian Rip the hessian away from the wall, then soak off the backing paper. This may take some time. Take care if the plaster is in poor condition, or you could pull the plaster off as well.

Lincrustas These materials are stuck in place with very strong adhesive and are hard to remove. Use hot water and a scraper to ease away the sheet from the wall, taking care not to pull away the plaster. Then soak and remove any remaining adhesive.

Cork wall tiles Use a flexible scraper with force to lift away the tiles, then soak the adhesive or use a hot air stripper to soften the remaining adhesive. Take care not to damage the wall plaster.

Ceiling coverings

If you hire a steam stripper to use on your ceilings, protect your eyes, head and hands from the very hot water. The domestic steam stripper is safer because the main water container holds only cold water, and steam is only produced at the face plate. All ceiling papers and vinyls are removed in the same way as wallcoverings.

Expanded polystyrene tiles Use a flexible scraper to lift tiles away, then use a hot air stripper to soften the adhesive before removing it with a scraper. Be sure to protect your eyes, hands and hair.

A domestic steam stripper is safest for stripping ceilings because it holds cold water and steam is only produced at the face plate

Many vinyl papers are easy to strip as the vinyl pulls away, leaving the backing paper intact on the wall: loosen a bottom corner, then pull one strip away, holding the vinyl out from the wall as shown

If the backing paper is in good condition and you are intending to repaper, you can leave the backing on the walls. Repaste loose seams and sand rough areas lightly. Backing paper is not suitable for painting over

WHY STRIP PAINT?

If paintwork is in good condition, it is best not to strip it, but there are exceptions. For example, paint may have built up to the point that windows and doors will not open properly – this is particularly noticeable on sash window frames. Painted surfaces may have taken on a treacle-like look where architraves and mouldings have lost their fine detail. This often happens when decorative ceiling roses have been emulsioned too many times.

You may have to strip paint in order to use one of the new microporous finishes which need to be in direct contact with bare wood. Be cautious about stripping back wood in order to stain and varnish, as quite a lot of sanding is necessary to remove all of the primer from the pores of the wood. If any remains, staining will be patchy.

It is wise to strip paint from radiators before repainting, as they will lose efficiency if too many paint layers build up. Special radiator paints are available which do not discolour when heated.

Lead danger

Never rub down old paintwork. It may contain lead which you would inhale. Do not use abrasives at all to remove paint. The friction softens the paint and clogs the abrasive, making it useless. Only use abrasives after stripping.

Dry scraping is possible using a skarsten scraper for convex surfaces like banister hand rails.

Be sure to protect your eyes and hands and wear a simple face mask when removing old paints.

Chemical stripping

This is expensive when large areas are involved. The secret is to be patient while the chemical works – otherwise you may need more coats to get to bare wood or metal. Protect your eyes and hands, and keep the stripper away from plastic items.

There are two main types of chemical stripper: first, a liquid which you apply with a brush and scrape away when the paint bubbles

Paint liquid stripper liberally over the surface to be stripped

Allow plenty of time for the chemical to work before you scrape away the paint

and breaks up; second, a paste which you trowel on and allow to set before you lift it away with the point of the trowel. The latter is best for mouldings and textured surfaces as it lifts paint out of hollows.

Be sure to neutralize the stripper after use, following the manufacturer's instructions.

You can send large items to specialist companies for stripping.

Using heat

Most paints soften quickly when you apply heat, but take great care as it is possible to ignite paint. Make sure there is no newspaper on the floor which might catch alight, and have a bucket of water handy into which you can drop ignited paint. Always hold the scraper in such a position

that no stripped paint can fall on your hand. Cotton gloves are useful.

Blowtorch This is powered by liquid gas, either from a small container attached to the torch head, or a larger container connected to the torch by a tube. The flame can be quite fierce, so keep it moving to avoid burning the wood. Always keep it well away from glass.

Hot air gun This resembles a powerful hair dryer, providing a jet of air heated by an electric element. It is safer than a blowtorch in that there is no flame, but this can be deceptive as you cannot see anything emerging from the gun. It can get hot enough to char wood and crack glass, so take just as much care as with a blowtorch. You can buy a deflector to control the heat.

Be careful not to char wood when you are using a hot air gun to strip paint from wood. Do not use it on or close to window frames – the heat can crack the glass panes

OUTSIDE WORK

Careful maintenance of the exterior of your home is vital if you are to keep the weather out; neglect can be a very costly business in the long term. Before decorating the outside of your home, spend time repairing and preparing exterior surfaces so that the new decorative coatings will look good and last longer.

Roof

Ideally you should start at the very top. A pair of binoculars is a useful aid: from gutter level you should check the ridge tiles to see that they are all in place, firmly bedded in mortar. If you decide to rebed them and are happy on the roof, hire a roof ladder. (*See page 25, Hiring Equipment.*) Use a ready-mixed mortar to which you add 1 part PVA adhesive to every 5 parts mixing water. This improves adhesion.

Flashings

Check the flashings – these are the strips which bridge the gaps between masonry and roof. You can make repairs with a special self-adhesive flashing strip. A special primer is supplied with the strip to ensure good bonding.

Is the chimney stack sound and the pots firmly bedded in mortar (flaunching)? Chimney work is best left to the experts as special scaffolding is needed and the masonry involved is extremely heavy.

Gutters

Use a stiff brush and trowel to clear the gutters of all debris.

Check metal guttering for signs of rust. Clean rusted areas with a wire brush and treat them with a rust-inhibitor or metal primer (you should wear safety specs for this job). If you find holes, repair them with an epoxy-resin paste filler. However, if the gutters are in really poor shape you should replace them. If you are moving cast iron this is always a two-person job because of the weight involved.

Check for loose gutter brackets. You may need to resite screw holes or, in some cases, replace rotten fascia boards. Check also the joints between gutter sections. Remove any loose seal here and reseal with gutter sealant.

If the gutters do need replacing, consider using plastic. It is easy to handle, is unaffected by the weather and needs no painting. When planning your order of outside work, remember that you should paint the fascia boards before new guttering is fixed in place.

Plastic guttering will need little treatment, though it is worth checking the joints from time to time to see that the seals are sound. These will be rubber or neoprene, and will occasionally need replacing.

1 On brickwork dig out loose and crumbling mortar to a depth of 12mm (½in), then brush clean before repointing with a ready-mixed mortar mix.

2 Just before applying the mortar, dampen the joints. Press the mix into the spaces between bricks. Finish by angling the trowel to make sloping joints.

Above: *A rough-cast effect can be created on brick, breeze or concrete walls with the use of a Tyrolean machine. This applicator sprays a mix of fine cement on to the wall when you turn the handle. It should be used on top of a dry undercoat rendering. The applicator can be hired*
Right: *It can also be used on internal walls*

Cladding

Examine timber cladding and remove all loose and flaking varnish or paint. Fill any holes and cracks with epoxy wood repair paste or exterior matching stopping. Seal any gaps between the boards, or between the boards and the walls, with an exterior flexible sealant. This will allow for any slight movement of the timber.

Plastic cladding needs an occasional wash down with warm soapy water to remove grime. Allow to dry naturally to prevent static.

Windows

Check for gaps around the frames. Clean out all loose material and fill with an exterior flexible sealant, pressing it well in and smoothing with a wet rag or finger.

Examine the paintwork and decide whether it needs stripping. Check the putty carefully for cracks, especially where the putty and glass meet. This is where the rain gets in and rots timber frames. Slight cracks can be sealed with a silicone rubber clear sealant, but if the putty is badly cracked dig it out, clean the rebates and apply new putty. Use metal casement putty or dual purpose putty on metal frames. (*See page 38, Sundries.*)

Doors

Treat frames as for windows. You may need to strip down naturally-finished timber doors to remove old finish, especially if linseed oil has been used. Do not reapply this – use an exterior allweather varnish instead. Seal cracks between the panels with an epoxy wood repair paste or exterior grade stopping.

Metal window frames or other metalwork in good condition can be given a coat of fast-drying metal primer. If the surface is rusty, sand back any flaking rust before applying the primer. When the primer is completely dry, cover it with your chosen shade of paint

Plastic gutters need no painting and are unaffected by weather conditions. Check the joints from time to time, however, to make sure that the seals are sound. If these show any signs of deterioration, apply a roof and gutter sealant direct from the dispenser tube

Use a stiff brush and trowel to clear metal gutters of debris. Clean any rusted areas with a stiff wire brush and treat with metal primer or a rust inhibitor. Fill holes with an epoxy-based repair paste. Treat bare metal with primer before applying new paint. Undercoat is not usually necessary

1 On old and rotting window frames, dig the surface with a penknife blade. If the blade sinks in then the wood is rotten. Use a narrow chisel to dig out the rotten wood, lifting it away. In small areas apply a wood hardener.

2 Apply wood hardener generously, dabbing it into the wood. It will strengthen the fibres. For extra protection drill a number of holes about 5mm (¼in) in diameter in surrounding wood and tip hardener into them.

3 Make good with a two-part wood repair paste. Following the instructions, mix the paste until it is a uniform colour. Fill the holes using a small trowel or filling knife. Leave the filler just proud of the surface. Sand back.

EXTERIOR WALL MAINTENANCE

Facing brick You should never paint attractive brickwork, for once paint soaks into brick it can never be cleaned off. Scrub it down instead with a stiff yard broom or clean it with a high pressure water jet.

Dig out loose and crumbling mortar to a depth of 12 mm (½ in), brush clean and repoint using a ready-mix mortar. Make the mix with the minimum of water so it is of sandpie consistency; this way you will keep the face of the brickwork clean. Damp the joints just before applying the new mortar. Smooth with a trowel to make flat or sloping joints, or with a piece of bent copper tube to produce hollow joints.

Rendering Check the paintwork on cement-rendered walls by running your hand over the surface. If it comes away covered in a chalky deposit, brush off loose and flaking material, then treat with a fungicide to kill mould. Finally, apply a stabilizing solution to bond on any remaining old finish. Wear safety specs for this job.

Look for minor cracks, rake out all loose material and fill with an exterior filler. For larger areas, rake out, damp and fill with mortar mix.

Check over outside walls which are coated with cement rendering by moving your hand over the surface. Brush away any loose material with a stiff-bristled brush

You can improve adhesion by adding PVA adhesive to the mixing water in a ratio of one part adhesive to five parts water. Keep the mix dry, but damp the area to be filled just before applying the mortar. If you find serious cracking, seek expert advice.

Dashed finishes Pebbledash and spar dash are best cleaned with a pressure hose then coated with stabilizing solution to help bind any loose material. Small areas may be repaired by cleaning out the damaged area, filling the hole with mortar, then throwing the displaced stones back into the mortar.

Treat good areas of cement rendering with a stabilizing solution to bond on the old finish. It is important always to wear safety specs for this job

Barge and fascia boards The barge boards are those which cover the ends of the roof and climb right up to the ridge. If you need to replace them, there is a special rigid foam-plastic board available which will not rot or need painting.

The fascia boards hold the gutters and cover the ends of roof timbers. Take down plastic guttering to decorate the fascias thoroughly.

Use epoxy resin wood repair material or one of the exterior wood stoppings to fill cracks and holes.

Damp-proof course

Walls can be affected by damp if paths or patios are too close to the damp-proof course level. There should be at least 150mm (6in) between ground-level and the damp-proof course so that rain does not splash above the damp-resisting barrier.

If possible, lower the ground level. Otherwise apply a skirting of mortar with an added waterproofer. This may bridge the damp-proof course but it must be in tight contact with the wall to keep out water. Ensure that heaped soil does not bridge the damp-proof course.

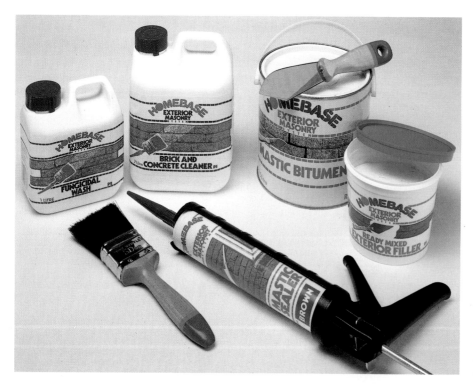

When repairing and cleaning a house exterior, pick materials that are specially designed for exterior use

REPAIRING ROTTEN WOOD

If you find areas of paintwork where there are hollows in the wood surface, or paint has flaked away, dig the surface with the point of a penknife blade. If the blade sinks into the wood with little or no resistance, the wood is rotten, and there is no point in redecorating until it has been repaired.

Dig into the rotten wood again with a narrow chisel, lifting out the soft, damaged timber until firmer wood is encountered.

Drying out

If the area is small, prise out all crumbling wood, and remove any traces of old paint or varnish. Then, if the area feels damp, use a hot air gun or blowtorch to dry the wood. If you are working near glass, shield it from the heat with a piece of hardboard or sheet metal.

Hardening

When dry, apply proprietary wood hardener. Be generous, allowing it to soak into the wood fibres and dabbing it in with a brush. For extra protection you can drill a number of holes, about 5mm (¼in) in diameter, in nearby wood, and tip hardener into them. It will only take about six hours to set, and will strengthen any soft fibres and prevent the ingress of more damp.

Filling

Next use a two-part wood repair paste to fill the hole. Check the instructions for the ratio of catalyst in one tube to repair paste in the other. Remember that when both are mixed, setting cannot be stopped. Mix well until it is of uniform colour, then fill the hole using a small trowel or filling knife, leaving the filler just proud of the surface. It will be hard enough to smooth with glasspaper in about 20 minutes – though in hot weather this time could be halved.

Do not mix more than you can use in a few minutes.

Smoothing down

When hard, use fine glasspaper to smooth the filler flush with the surrounding surface. Always work with the grain of the wood to avoid scratch marks across the grain.

If you plan to paint the area, any two-part woodfiller will do, but if you wish to stain and natural-finish with a seal or varnish, be sure you buy a filler which will take stain. Some will not – with these you would get ugly blotches where the filler had been used, which are impossible to hide.

To protect vulnerable areas, drill holes in the timber and insert and seal-in special wood preserving tablets. These will dissolve and release a powerful fungicide should the wood get damp.

Having made good the damaged area, check to see how it became damp in the first place. You may need to replace putty or re-seal around frames to keep damp out. (See page 45, Windows.)

Replacing wood

If the damaged area is greater than is practical to fill, plan to cut out the damaged timber and replace it with new. Use a chisel, mallet and tenon saw to remove all the damaged wood and shape the remaining wood so that you can match it with new wood. Apply wood hardener to any remaining soft fibres. Treat exposed wood with a clear wood preservative and, if you are planning to paint, use pre-treated timber to fill the hole. Otherwise, treat your shaped piece with clear wood preservative before you fit it in place. It is best to cut your repair piece slightly too high so you can smooth it back later to the required level.

Drill your repair wood to take rustless screws, and bore holes about 6mm (¼in) deep into which the heads of your screws can sink. Apply a liberal coating of waterproof wood adhesive, then screw the piece of wood in place. Fill the screw holes with two-part wood filler, and leave the filler to harden.

Finishing off

When the adhesive has set, smooth any projecting wood with glasspaper until it is flush with the surrounding areas. Unless you have been very accurate, you may find slight gaps in places between old and new timber. If so, fill the gaps with wood repair paste, allow to set, then smooth with glasspaper. You could use a wood stopping for this filling work, but if you do, be sure it is a weatherproof grade. Always use the correct mix: interior fillers should never be used for exterior repairs.

If damage is extensive you may need a joiner to effect major repairs. If you find wood has dried out and crumbled and there are signs of whitish strands and a musty smell, suspect dry rot.

1 To protect wood around doors and windows, drill holes in the timber wide enough for you to insert special wood preserving tablets. If the wood becomes damp these release a fungicide

2 Next fill the holes with an exterior grade wood filler. Push the filler well into the holes, clean up with a scraper or filling knife but leave the filler proud of the surface of the holes. Sand back when dry

PAINTING

When all the preparatory work has been done you can start putting on the new paint. Stir the paint you have chosen thoroughly, using either a clean, smooth piece of wood or a stirring rod fitted to a power drill. If you use power, remember never to lift the rod out of the paint while the drill is turning!

Stir with a lifting motion to raise any sediment from the base of the can. Then, if you are using liquid paint, pour some into a paint kettle. The reason for this is that should paint become contaminated in any way, only that in your kettle will be affected.

For emulsion paint you will need a paint tray into which a quantity of paint can be tipped. You will not need a tray if you are using a solid emulsion – it can be taken straight from the tray it comes in.

Wear clothes which will not shed hairs. Lint-free coveralls are ideal. Professional decorators wear white overalls but you can also buy an inexpensive version.

CEILINGS

The first essential for painting a ceiling is to form a simple platform, which could be made from a pair of steps, a stout wooden box and a scaffold board. Arrange it so your head is about 75mm (3in) from the ceiling. You can work from just a pair of steps, but it involves a lot more tiring legwork as you have to keep climbing up and down to move the steps.

Remember that you can leave old wallpaper in place while the ceiling is being decorated – any splashes will be removed with the paper later.

Your choice of decorating tools will depend on the texture of the ceiling. For a smooth surface, use a brush, foam roller, mohair roller or paint pad; for deep texture and for rough surfaces use either a brush or a shaggy pile roller.

If you choose a brush, use the widest you can handle comfortably. Work it in all directions, and use a dabbing motion to fill crevices in textured surfaces.

With a roller, again work in all directions – not too fast, or paint will be flung off. Let the roller shed all its paint before recharging it. Do not paint too thick a coating – in most cases two thin coats are ideal. Work the roller across the direction of the first coat when applying your second to fill in the bits missed first time.

Work in all directions with a paint pad. This will only apply a thin coat, but most emulsion dries quickly so you can soon add further coats.

If you use either a roller or a paint pad, you may find you need a small paintbrush to finish off in corners and close to walls where the other tools could not quite reach. Brush out well to blend the paint in.

When you are sure the ceiling is complete, it is time to strip the walls. (*See page 42, Stripping.*) Get into the habit of packing stripped paper into bin liners as work progresses so that reactivated paste does not stick to the floor and you do not tread paper into the rest of the house.

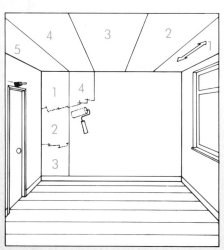

Order of painting a room
a *Ceiling, starting at window end, 1-5*
b *Prime and undercoat frames and doors*
c *Paint walls, large wall surfaces first, 1-4 and so on*
d *Frames, top coat*
e *Doors, top coat*
f *Floor, if you are painting*

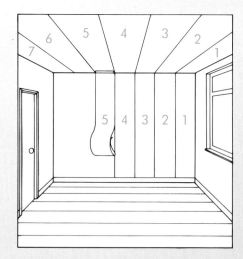

Order of painting and papering a room
a *Paper or paint ceiling, starting at window end, 1-7*
b *Complete all painting*
c *Paper walls, starting at window end, 1-5 and so on*
d *Floor, if you are painting*

INTERIOR WALLS

After stripping walls, and before you have a final clean-up, check that the walls are smooth, and give a light rub over with a sandpaper block where necessary. Lift any remaining newspaper, sweep up any debris and vacuum to pick up fine dust. Lay fresh newspaper around the walls to keep splashes off the floor.

Use masking tape around light switches and any fitting which cannot be removed from the walls. If you are not going to repaint the door and window frames, run strips of masking tape around the edges where the brush or roller may otherwise touch them.

Remember to remove all masking tape before the paint hardens, otherwise you will rip the paint away with the tape.

If you are using a brush, choose the widest you can comfortably handle. Start at the top of a wall and run bands of paint downwards, leaving a slight gap between the bands. Then brush across the wall to blend the bands together, finishing with light, vertical strokes. Do not apply too much paint at once – two thin coats are always better than one thick one.

If you decide to use a roller, the type you need will depend on the texture of the wall surface. Use a foam or mohair roller for smooth surfaces and well-rounded textures, and a shaggy pile roller for deeply textured and rough surfaces. Initially you can work the roller in all directions, then finish off with light strokes in one direction. Do not try to cover more than about 1 sq m (yd) at a time.

You can also use a paint pad in all directions. Remember the pad applies only a very thin coat of emulsion – expect to put on two or even three coats if you have an under-colour to hide.

Whatever tool you use, you will probably need a small paintbrush to finish off in corners and at edges which can be awkward to reach.

CLEAN WORK

If you plan to use a number of colours of paint, line your paint kettle or roller tray with layers of kitchen foil, pressing it well into the shape of the container. Then, when one colour is complete, you can merely remove the top layers of foil and the container is ready to accept a second colour.

Where possible use a different brush for each colour to save time cleaning brushes.

When you have done the preparatory work (*see pages 39-47, Preparation*), wipe over all surfaces to be painted with a damp lint-free rag to remove any fine dust.

If woodwork surfaces are bare, you will need to apply wood primer to seal them. When they are dry, rub down very lightly, dust them off, then apply undercoat. It is undercoat that gives body to the coating. The top coat merely protects, unless you use a paint combining undercoat and top coat.

If the paint is sound and rubbed down, you will not need primer. Use as many coats of undercoat as you need to lose sight of a heavy colour. If you are re-painting with the same colour you can miss out the undercoat and just apply top coat.

Picture rails

Brush on paint along the run of the rail, and use a paint shield to keep it off the wall. Alternatively, if the wall paint has been dry for a long time, use masking tape where the rail and wall meet, then remove the tape before the paint hardens.

Skirting board

Use the same technique as for picture rails. Move a sheet of card along the floor to ensure that your brush does not pick up dirt from under the skirting board. (*See picture below.*)

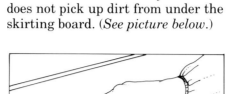
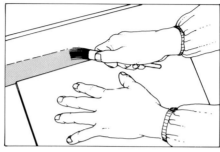

Coving

Whatever type of coving you have you will need to use emulsion paint, and the decision is yours as to whether this matches the walls or ceiling or is in a contrasting colour. The usual way is to match the ceiling colour. Use a paint shield or masking tape for a neat finish; alternatively stencil a design on the coving or add a decorative strip. (*See page 68, Decorative Ideas.*)

Switch plates

In older homes you may find switches mounted on timber plates raised away from the wall. These can be painted to complement the rest of the paintwork; use masking tape to keep the paint off the wall. If you wish to disguise the switches cover with emulsion paint in the same colour as used on the walls.

If you are going to paper the walls the painting technique is different. Take a band of paint about 12mm (½in) wide on to the walls adjoining the rails, skirtings and frames so that no bare wall will be seen if the paper does not come right up to the paintwork.

STORING PAINT

Transfer small amounts of paint left in the cans to small, screw-top jars which the paint will just fill. It will keep almost indefinitely this way, and can be used for touching up damaged areas. Left in large cans it will soon dry up.

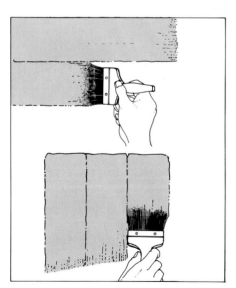

When using a brush to paint walls choose a wide brush and coat it liberally with paint. Apply, starting from the top of the wall and working in horizontal bands. When using matt emulsion finish off with criss-cross strokes; when working with satin emulsion use light, upward strokes to spread the paint

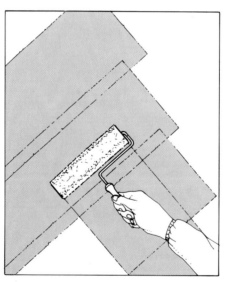

When using a roller pour some paint into the tray, dip in the roller and run it up and down the tray slope to distribute the paint evenly. Run the roller over the wall in a criss-cross pattern, being careful to merge joins and fill in any gaps. Finish off by using a small brush around wall edges for a neat finish

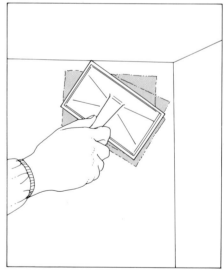

When using a paint pad decant some paint into a tray and draw the pad across the surface, removing any excess on the side. Smooth paint on in a criss-cross pattern, in the same way as when using a paint roller, again being careful to merge all join lines. Paint pads are especially useful for running along wall edges

INTERIOR DOORS AND WINDOWS

Although there are no strict rules for painting doors and windows, there is a logical sequence for each – which you will find illustrated below. In all cases, remove as many fittings as possible – door handles, escutcheon plates, window stays, and so on. The ideal way to paint a door is laid flat, so if you can unhinge it and lay it over two trestles, painting will be that much easier.

Pad the trestles with old rags or magazines so that you do not damage the underside of the door.

Select paint brushes carefully to suit the surface to be painted. Use your widest brush for a flush door, and your smallest for the decorative moulding of a panelled door.

With all doors, paint the edge away from the hinges last of all so that you have something to hold on to until the final moments.

If you wish to shut the windows at night, paint them early in the morning so that they have the maximum amount of time to dry. Set masking tape back 3mm (⅛in) on the glass so that just a thin ribbon of paint goes on to the glass. This line of paint seals the joint between the glass and the frame which is where damp so often finds a way in.

Panelled doors
First paint the mouldings around the panels (**1**), then paint the panels themselves (**2**). Begin each panel at the top and start with upper panels. Continue by coating the centre vertical next to the panels (**3**), then the three horizontal rails starting from the top (**4**). Follow by completing the outer vertical strips and then do all the door edges (**5**). Finish by painting the complete door frame (**6**).

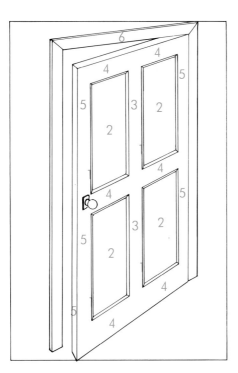

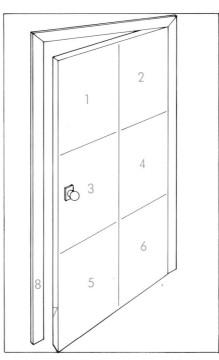

Flush doors
These need to be broken up into small sections for ease. Paint each side of the door quickly to avoid tide marks. Use a 75mm (3 in) wide brush and start at a top corner, working on an approximate square half the width of the door. Begin with vertical strokes, then brush across these and finish with light, upward strokes (**1**). Complete each numbered section in the same way. Use a small brush to complete the edges (**7**). Finish with the frame (**8**).

Sash windows
Push the rear sash down and the front sash up so that at least 20cm (8in) of the lower rear sash is exposed. Paint the bottom rail of the rear sash and any upright exposed sections (**1**). Pull the rear sash up and almost shut and paint the rest (**2**). Paint the front sash slightly open (**3**). When dry, paint the frame, shut the window and paint the exposed part of the runners. Do not get paint on the cords. Finally paint the sill (**4**).

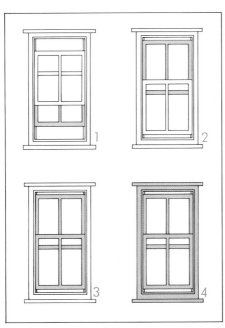

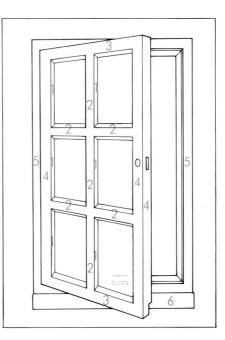

Casement windows
First paint the rebates (**1**), then move on to do the horizontal and vertical crossrails (**2**). Do the horizontal top and bottom sides and edges next (**3**), then the vertical sides and edges (**4**). When the window is dry, paint the complete frame including the edges (**5**). Leave the sill until almost last to avoid smudging this while working (**6**). Leave the stay, if this needs painting, until last so you can use it.

DECORATING A STAIRWELL

The top of a stairwell is the most difficult area to reach, and you will need some form of scaffolding. You can hire a staircase platform which will fit neatly on the stairs by means of adjustable legs. Alternatively, if you do not mind heights, lean a ladder against the stairwell wall so the base sits in the angle between tread and riser. Rest a scaffold board on a suitable rung of the ladder, then make a support at the other end from a stout wooden box or small pair of steps so that the board lies horizontally. (*See picture, right.*)

If you are painting walls, you can use a roller with extension pole which slots into the handle, or a paint pad with a similar facility.

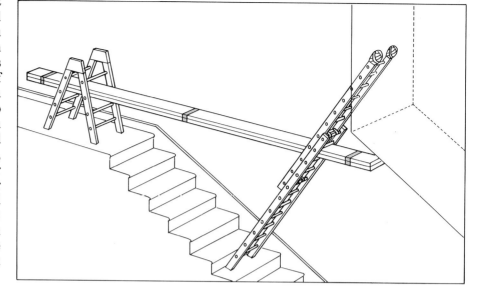

EXTERIOR PAINTING

Painting the outside of a home can seem a very daunting task. However, if you consider that it does not all have to be completed in one session, it begins to look like a more manageable proposition.

Some faces of the house will weather more than others, depending upon aspect and prevailing winds, so you can do the sheltered aspects less often. Each face of your home can be broken down into easily tackled areas – one complete door or window, or a particular wall surface, so that the whole job is divided into sections, with the work spread over weeks or months.

Whatever way you decide to tackle it, make sure you never leave bare surfaces. Always apply a protective coating before work stops so the weather cannot get in.

Wherever possible, cover areas like porch roofs, tiled sills and decorative paving to avoid splashing. If you should splash, clean up while the paint is still wet.

Access

Make sure that access to the area to be decorated is easy and safe. Erect the ladder at the correct angle – 1 metre (3ft) out for every 4 metres (13ft) up – and anchor it top and bottom so it cannot move. If you are using a scaffold tower, make sure it is standing firmly and immovably. Ideally, anchor it to the house.

If you are working at gutter level, arrange for the ladder to extend at least three rungs above gutter level so there is always a good hand grip. Never work with your arms above the end of the ladder. Access above a sun room is often difficult if the roof is glazed. It may be possible to stand a ladder either side of the extension, fit two cripple supports then lay a scaffold board across. However, you will need to be extremely careful as there will be nothing for you to hold on to.

For bungalow work, most areas can be reached from a stepladder. For convenience, ideally use one with a tray on which you can rest paint and accessories.

Making light work

Make sure exterior paints are well mixed. The use of a paint kettle is even more important where there is the possibility of contamination by crumbling mortar or masonry.

Where wall areas are so large that you may not be able to complete the whole job at once, try to divide the work into manageable sections by using windows, doors and perhaps cladding as dividers.

It helps to fit a stand-off to the top of the ladder for work on walls and gutters. This lifts the top section away from the wall for clearance, and also makes the ladder less likely to slide sideways when not anchored at the top.

WALLS

You should have already carried out any necessary repair work on exterior walls (*see page 44, Outside Work*), but give the wall surfaces a final examination before applying any new decoration. The main cause of failure of exterior paints is poor preparation.

Smooth rendering Check for discoloration caused by mould growth. Treat mould, however light, covering the whole wall surface with a fungicide diluted as recommended. Protect your eyes and hands, and follow all the recommendations on the container.

Rub your hand over any existing paintwork. If it leaves a chalky deposit, you need to seal the surface or your new finish will flake away from the wall. Treat the wall with a stabilizing solution which will bond the chalking material to the wall.

Decorate the wall with a good exterior masonry paint, using either

PAINTING EXTERNAL WINDOWS

a large brush or a shaggy nylon exterior roller. A medium-to-soft dustpan brush is an ideal brush applicator. Use it to lay on and stipple-in the paint. Do not try to spread paint too far. You may need two coats to hide an under-colour.

With a roller, control the speed of application so paint does not fly. If you do get splashes, clean them up while they are still wet.

With either tool, start at the top of the wall and work down, taking in areas of about 1 sq m (yd) at a time.

Dash finishes Check for mould growth and chalking as for smooth rendering and treat accordingly. Then use either a brush or an exterior grade shaggy nylon roller to apply paint. With deep textures, you may find a check-over with a brush necessary to stipple-in paint in areas the roller could not reach.

You will need about twice as much paint for deeply-textured surfaces as for smooth.

Decorative brickwork Do not be tempted to paint attractive facing brickwork – it does not look good, and once applied is virtually impossible to remove. Instead, wash it with a proprietary brick cleaner after damping down the wall with clean water. Do not use detergents to clean. They leave marks on the brick when the water dries. To brighten brickwork further you could also repoint using a lighter mortar mix.

If the brickwork seems too porous, apply a coat of silicone waterproofing liquid to it when it is dry. This will prevent the ingress of water while still allowing the brickwork to breathe. However, take care to keep silicones off glass – silicone leaves marks.

Decorative stonework Treat as for brick, using a proprietary stone cleaner to remove grime. Like brick, stonework is best not painted, but should you wish to change the colour, use a proprietary stone paint, avoiding the mortar joints.

Top: Sand frames to provide a key for new paint. **Above:** *Protect window glass from paint splashes with masking tape*

Before you start painting windows, check that gaps between frames and masonry have been properly sealed with a sealant (*see page 45*). Check that all putty is sound, with no cracks, especially between the glass and the putty. To make painting easier, apply masking tape to the glass leaving just a 3mm (⅛in) of glass close to the frames showing. This will ensure that just enough paint goes on to the glass to seal the joint between glass and putty. The alternative is to use a paint shield.

Timber frames

If you are using traditional paints on wood, you need to seal any visible knots with patent knotting to prevent resin bleeding out in warm weather. Then apply primer to seal the pores of the wood, followed by undercoat and at least two coats of gloss finish. Choose a brush just a little narrower than the surface being painted, and finish brushing along the longest surfaces, which is usually with the grain of the wood.

If you prefer to use a microporous finish, you will need to use one or two special paints depending upon the system you choose. The paint goes on to bare wood. You should not apply more than two coats or the microporous effect will be limited. Brush out as for standard paint.

If you are re-covering existing paintwork which has been prepared (*see page 40, Windows*), you will not need to apply primer. You will only need undercoat if there is a change of colour. Remember that gloss coats have little or no obliterative powers. You can use microporous paint over existing paint, but it loses its valuable breathing quality.

See page 51, Painting Windows, for the order of painting window frames. If you get splashes on the glass, allow them to dry then remove them with a razor blade.

Metal frames

If the frames are galvanized, choose a calcium plumbate primer if you plan to paint them with standard undercoat and gloss. The alternative is to use a paint specially formulated for coating galvanized surfaces or alloys. This is like an enamel, and you can apply it directly to the galvanizing, providing a fast-drying gloss surface. You can also use it on aluminium frames if you so wish. You will not need an undercoat.

Never apply too much paint on metal or you will get runs. It is far better to apply two thin coats.

If you have sash windows, do not allow paint to get on the sash cords. It makes the rope brittle.

When exterior painting is complete, check that there are no splashes on tiled sills, then paint them with a special tile paint. If the mortar between the tiles looks new and attractive, do not paint it; otherwise take the paint on to the mortar.

EXTERNAL DOORS

A painted door adds bright colour to plain white surroundings

A stained and sealed finish shows off a hardwood door

Painting

If a door is over-tight in its frame, it may have too many coats of paint. If so, strip back those surfaces which meet the door frame. Look for any fine cracks around the panels where the wood has shrunk. Check the advice on preparation. (*See page 40.*)

Treat knots in timber with patent knotting to seal in the resin, which may be exuded in hot weather. Apply wood primer, undercoat and at least two top coats of exterior quality paint. Follow the correct sequence of painting. (*See page 51.*)

Do not overload your brush when painting mouldings or you will get runs, but do ensure that all the points of the mouldings are covered.

Work your final brush strokes with the longest run of the wood, which is usually with the wood grain, and choose brushes to suit the width of wood being painted.

A painted door in good condition may only need an extra top coat of gloss, but if you wish to change the colour use an undercoat.

A painted galvanized steel garage door

Natural finishes

Great advances have been made in the formulation of varnishes and seals, and if they are correctly applied there should be no trouble with flaking or peeling. However, do choose a material designed for exterior use. For preference, this should be microporous, contain a fungicide to protect the finish against mould growth as well as an ultraviolet filter to counter the bleaching effects of the sun.

These finishes must go on to bare wood, and you can either leave the wood its natural colour or stain it. This can be done with a wood stain or dye, or a finish containing a stain. Apply two or three thin coats, brushing them out well and allowing each to dry before the next is applied. Where necessary, use a fine glasspaper between coats to smooth the finish. Dust well before applying the next coat.

Painting alloy frame

If you wish to paint an aluminium door surround, use a special paint designed for use on alloys. It needs no primer or undercoat, though you may need two coats.

Treat garage doors as larger versions of standard doors and follow the same basic painting technique, using the largest brush you can comfortably handle.

Paint galvanized metal doors with a special paint for this purpose. You will not need primer or undercoat.

GUTTERS AND DRAINPIPES

Gutters

The type of gutters you have will determine how much decorating you have to do. Modern plastic gutters and down-pipes need no painting, and it is a simple job to take down the gutters if the fascia boards holding them are in need of attention. Remember that you cannot heat-strip near plastics without causing damage.

If you want to paint older plastic guttering, use a good quality exterior gloss direct on to the plastic, but it is unlikely that you will need to repaint newer plastic guttering.

Metal guttering is more likely to need decorating. First remove all dust and debris from inside and then rinse down with clean water. Watch how the water flows away to the down-pipes. If it gathers anywhere en route, you may need to adjust the brackets to ensure a free flow.

Look for signs of rusting. Wire-brush away all loose material and coat the damaged area with a rust-inhibiting paint.

If you find actual holes, clean away all damaged material and seal the holes with an epoxy-based repair paste. This consists of paste and hardener which, when mixed, set chemically to form a tough material which inhibits rust.

Examine all joints in the guttering. You may find the sealant has gone hard and has perhaps dropped out. Dig out all loose and damaged material, brush clean then reseal with a gutter-sealing mastic. Smooth the mastic on the inside of the gutter with a wet finger so that there is no projection to obstruct the flow of water.

Where a joint is in poor condition, undo the holding bolts, separate the sections and remake the joint with gutter sealant.

Treat any spots of bare metal with metal priming paint, then, if the paintwork is in good condition, apply new paint. You will not need to use an undercoat unless you are changing the colour. Where you find you are back to bare metal, use metal primer, undercoat and at least

Top: Remove all loose debris from gutters before examining them for signs of wear
Above: Sand rust spots and prime bare areas of metal before repainting

two top coats of paint.

This is a good opportunity to use up any left-over exterior gloss paint on the inside of the gutters where it cannot be seen.

If you find the paint fails to dry properly, or that colour bleeds through, it may indicate that bituminous paint was used on the gutters. In this case bituminous paint should be used for repainting. When applying paint to gutters and down-pipes, hold a piece of card behind to keep the paint off other surfaces.

When you have finished the painting, fit a plastic cage over the mouth of each downpipe. This will prevent birds from nesting there. Nesting birds frequently cause blockages in downpipes.

Gutter netting is a mixed blessing. It can keep leaves out of the gutters, but, if there are a lot of them, the leaves can coat the netting when wet and prevent rainwater from draining into the gutters.

Downpipes

These are usually painted in a similar fashion to gutters, as they are probably of the same material. Check downpipes for any rust and treat these areas with metal priming paint. Look for signs of damage at the joints. Never be tempted to seal the joints between sections of metal downpipe. Should the pipe become blocked, these will show you to the nearest section where the blockage has occurred.

If you encounter a crack – perhaps caused by refuse freezing and expanding in the pipe – use an epoxy resin repair paste plus a length of glassfibre bandage to make a repair. Apply some repair paste, wind the bandage into it, then apply more paste and leave to set. It can be painted within half an hour.

Painting the outside of the pipe is simple enough, but use a piece of card as a shield between the wall and the pipe while you paint the back. If the pipe is plastic, use a good quality exterior gloss paint direct on to the cleaned pipe. No primer or undercoat is needed.

Check the inside of cast iron downpipe with a torch, and, if it looks rusty, lengthen its life by coating it with bituminous paint. To paint inside the pipe you will need a thin, heavy weight, such as an old sash-cord weight, tied to a stout rope. Bind old towelling around the weight to make a plug which just slides inside the pipe top. Lower the plug in a little way, then tip in some paint. Work the plug up and down to spread the paint – and make sure you do not drop the weight down the pipe. This system only works on straight runs of pipe.

Do not use too much paint. Use just enough to spread on the pipe wall or you could restrict the flow at the base with congealed paint.

Having cleaned out the gulleys, now is a good time to take out and paint the grids, assuming they are metal. If they are rusty, sand back and use a rust-inhibiting paint, followed by exterior paint. Leave to dry before replacing them.

PAINTING CLADDING

Timber cladding

When you have prepared the timber for painting, examine the boards carefully for any gaps between them where rain could beat in. These gaps are often caused by shrinkage. Fill them with a flexible exterior grade sealant, which will be able to take up any slight seasonal movement. Check also along the bottom edge of the cladding – rain can be forced up here in high winds. Seal small gaps with flexible sealant and fill large gaps with an expanding foam filler, cutting away any surplus once the foam has expanded and set.

Before painting, ensure surrounding surfaces are protected with dust sheets.

If you are using a traditional painting system, prime all bare wood, then apply undercoat and top coat. Use at least two coats of gloss, finishing off with brush strokes along the length of the timber, and working paint well into the joints between the boards.

The alternative is to use a microporous paint, but this must go directly on to bare timber so any moisture trapped in the wood can escape through the microporous finish. This is available in white and a number of wood colours. Do not apply more than two coats.

An attractive cladding could enhance the appearance of the house by being natural-finished, but this involves careful stripping back to bare wood, making sure that all traces of primer are removed from the timber surface. This usually involves sanding back rather than stripping, so that a new layer of clean wood is exposed.

Make sure that all the joints between the boards are also free from old finish, for missed areas can result in a blotchy appearance if you are applying stain.

Next decide whether you are happy with the existing colour, or whether you would like to change it. If so, you have two options: you can either apply a wood stain, then use a clear protective finish, or you can use a decorative seal containing a stain. With a wood stain, you can apply any number of protective coats without much affecting the tone, but if you use a decorative coating containing stain, every additional coat will darken the wood further.

When applying the stain, make sure the edges of each brush stroke are still wet as you increase the stained area so that you do not get patchiness. If a water-based stain is used, smooth it down when dry, rubbing very lightly with a fine grade of glasspaper, and working only with the grain of the wood.

For the protective coating, make sure you choose an exterior-grade varnish or seal – ideally a microporous one containing a fungicide and an ultra-violet filter. Work the first coat well into the wood with a brush, applying only a thin coating. Then follow with a second coat applied a little thicker.

Apart from the seals, there are matt stain preservatives which protect the timber without imparting a gloss to it.

Plastic cladding

One of the advantages of plastic cladding is that it needs no decoration. A wash down with warm water containing a mild cleaning agent is all that is necessary.

Never use abrasives in any form, as they roughen the surface, which in turn will afford a grip for dirt and dust. Never polish the plastic with a dry duster. This often leads to a build-up of static electricity which will attract and hold dust.

If you do want to change the colour of plastic cladding, you can apply a good quality gloss paint direct to the cladding. You will not need primer or undercoat.

COMMON PAINT FAULTS

Modern paints from reputable manufacturers rarely give any trouble. The fault usually lies with the surface to which they are applied – or lack of careful preparation of the surface. The following are some of the most common faults:

Blistering *See picture, opposite page.*
Flaking Encountered where the paint has no grip on the undersurface. Perhaps it was too smooth – as with old gloss – or too chalky. Badly flaking areas are best stripped and redecorated.
Crazing *See picture, opposite page.*
Wrinkling If a second coat of paint is applied before the solvent has evaporated out of the first, wrinkling may occur. Strip back and redecorate, allowing each coat to harden before applying the next.

Plastic cladding is easy to maintain and does not need decorating with paint or stain. Wash it with warm soapy water from time to time to keep it clean and bright

Blistering occurs when air or water is trapped under the paint. Strip back paint

Crazing happens when incompatible paints are used. Rub smooth and recoat

Runs are the result of too much paint being applied. Scrape off when dry, then sand

Matt patches These often occur where a priming coat has not been used. Subsequent coats soak into the wood, resulting in a loss of gloss. Applying further coats rarely solves the problem – the only solution is to strip back and prime first.

Runs *See picture, above.*

Staining Often encountered when emulsion paint is put over a stained area and the stain bleeds through. Allow the emulsion to dry, then spray the affected area with a stain-sealer. This dries in a few minutes, and you can then paint over it.

Bleeding You will come across bleeding where wood contains knots which have not been sealed. The warmth of the sun encourages resin to bleed out, damaging the paint film. To correct, strip back the damaged area, treat the knots with patent knotting, and repaint.

Poor drying Usually caused by applying paint over a dirty or greasy surface. Strip back, clean and repaint.

Colour showing through Usually caused by lack of undercoat. Remember a top coat has little obliterative power. Rub down well, undercoat until the colour is hidden, then top coat.

Grittiness This is caused by dirt which has been picked up on the paint brush, and is especially common when you are exterior painting close to masonry. If the paint is still wet, you can simply wipe it off with a lint-free rag and repaint the area with a clean brush. If the paint is dry, rub it back with glasspaper and then repaint. If the paint in the can is contaminated, strain it.

Insects on paint If the paint is still wet, lift off the insects with a penknife or similar implement then smooth out the paint. If the paint is drying, leave well alone until the paint is hard, then rub away the insect with your finger.

BRUSHES AND PAINTS

When a brush has been cleaned and is still damp, slip an elastic band over the brush tip to hold the bristles together. Provided it is not too tight, this will ensure a good shape with no stray 'whiskers'. If there are still stray bristles when the elastic band is removed, snap them off at the stock with a penknife.

When they are dry, store brushes in a sealed polythene bag to keep them free from dust. Before using a brush again, flick the bristles back and forth against your hand, then twirl the brush by rolling the handle between your hands. This will dislodge loose bristles and bits.

Never use paint brushes for dusting off surfaces. Always keep a separate brush for this purpose.

Mark brushes which have been used for applying wood stains and keep them for similar jobs. (*See also pages 19 and 20, Cleaning and Storing Brushes.*)

PAINTS

Paint which has been stored for some time can be affected in two ways. First, a brownish liquid may have appeared, floating on the top. Disperse it by mixing, and make sure there is no sediment which needs stirring in.

Secondly, a skin may have formed on the surface. Carefully cut around this with a knife, scrape any paint from the underside of the skin and drop it back in the can. Strain the paint before use. You can either buy a paint strainer, or use a piece of washed nylon stocking. If you wish to use the paint from the paint can, fix the stocking loosely over the can with an elastic band, push the nylon down into the paint, and dip the brush into the nylon. The paint will seep up through it.

If you find an emulsion paint can has rusted inside, carefully transfer the paint into another container, discarding any emulsion which has been contaminated by rust.

USING WALLCOVERINGS

When all the painting is complete, prepare the room for applying the wallcovering. Give the walls and ceiling a final check over for any uneven filler or rough areas where old wallcovering has been removed and rub down with medium glasspaper where necessary.

Clean the room thoroughly, using a vacuum cleaner to pick up fine dust. Remove any old newspaper which you have spread over the floor while sanding and wipe skirtings, door and window frames with a damp rag to pick up any remaining dust. Lay fresh newspaper around the walls to catch splashes of size.

Always paper a ceiling before you paper the walls. If you are using a pasting table, position it so that it will not interfere with the area you plan to paper first. Ideally, when papering the walls, this will be a wall at right angles to the main window, and you will be starting close to the window and working away from it. Check how you will reach the highest point to paper. A short step-stool may be sufficient, otherwise use a small pair of steps. If the room has been newly plastered, the first job is to size the walls and ceiling. This fulfils a dual purpose: first, the size makes the wall more slippery so you will be able to slide your paper into place, and secondly, it improves adhesion. It will also act as a sealer, reducing the porosity of the wall surface.

Size may either be a separate material, bought as size powder and mixed with cold water, or it can be paste diluted as recommended on the packet. Separate size is generally stronger. Apply it to the walls and ceiling with your pasting brush, making sure you get into corners. Leave to dry before papering – normally this only takes an hour or so. Wash out the brush immediately.

If your wallcovering needs pasting, check what thickness of paste you need. The packet will advise quantities for all types of paper from light to heavy and, as a general rule, the heavier the paper, the less the water content of the paste should be. Stir the paste with a wooden spoon till smooth. Tubbed pastes need no preparation.

Sort out your rolls of wallcovering, making sure that the batch numbers are the same. Then remove the wraps from a number of rolls and check them against each other for colouring and shading. Should you find that they vary, use any odd rolls in places where a slight colour difference will not show.

If the paper has a clearly defined pattern, hold a roll against the top of the wall and decide what you want to see at the top – for example, if you have chosen a floral pattern you may want a whole flower to be visible rather than one cut in half. If the wall varies slightly in height along its length, however, careful positioning may highlight the fault, whereas an area of undefined pattern along the ceiling edge may act as a buffer.

The height of the wall to be papered may conflict with the pattern repeat so that quite a large piece needs trimming off the roll with each length to get a match. You can sometimes avoid as much waste by taking a length from another roll. This can make the difference between getting four full lengths rather than only three from a roll.

Save areas which need smaller pieces of paper until last – for example, under and above windows and around radiators. Some of your cut pieces will suffice here.

There are two ways of working with the kind of paper you have to paste. First, you can put up piece one, then match the paper still on the roll against it and mark top and bottom, allowing an extra 5cm (2in) top and bottom for trimming. Cut piece two, paste, hang and repeat the procedure. The second method is to measure and cut your first piece, lay it on the pasting table pattern-up, then match and cut your next piece against it.

The first method is safest with a defined pattern and where there is some discrepancy in wall height. The second method is quicker if walls are regular and the pattern simple to match. Roll each cut piece so the edge you can see represents the bottom of the piece.

Line impervious or damaged walls horizontally before hanging a heavy wallcovering. Lining paper must always be at right angles to the main wallcovering

PAPERING A CEILING

The first essential when papering a ceiling is to be able to reach it in reasonable comfort. You need a platform on which to stand so that your head is positioned about 7cm (3in) from the ceiling. Erect the platform along the line of the first piece of paper to be hung.

Size the ceiling first, and choose a thick paste which will hold the paper firmly once you have pressed it in place. The thinner the paste, the more readily the paper will drop away.

The best starting place is parallel with the main window wall. This ensures that no shadows will be thrown should there be any overlap of paper.

The simplest way to mark the position for your first length is to make a pencil mark on the ceiling at each end, the width of the ceiling paper away from the wall. If there is a crack to hide, deduct 5mm (¼in) so the paper will just turn on to the wall. If you have put up coving, this will have been dealt with.

Now rub a length of thin string with coloured chalk. Secure it to the ceiling at one end, immediately over the pencil mark; get a helper to hold the other end tightly to the other mark while you pluck the string to leave a line on the ceiling. Until you are really experienced, papering a ceiling is a two-person job – one person applying the paper while the other ensures that the applied paper stays in place.

 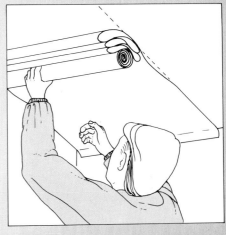

1 Measure for the first length of paper and add 10cm (4in) for trimming. Cut and lay the length on the table with the surplus on the floor to your left if you are right-handed. Paste as for wallpaper, draw the paper on to the table and fold over about ½ metre (1½ft). Fold again, concertina-wise, until fresh paper is in place for pasting. Continue to paste and fold until you have reached the end of the length.

2 Allow the paper to soak, then lay it over a spare roll of paper with the edge to be stuck first uppermost. Hold the roll in your left hand (if you are right-handed), grip the top edge with your right, turn it paste-side up and apply it to the corner where you plan to start. Slide it to the chalk line and smooth it on to the ceiling with your right hand.

3 Move along the platform and release a fold, keeping the roll close to the ceiling. Smooth the paper to the ceiling, then get your helper to hold the paper to the ceiling with a broom while you move along, releasing more folds and smoothing. (*See pages 58 and 59, main picture.*)

4 Continue papering until the length is up. Check over it with your smoothing brush, ensuring that the edges are well stuck down.

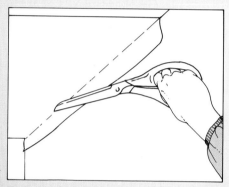

5 Press the paper into the end walls. Crease with the blunt edge of your scissors.

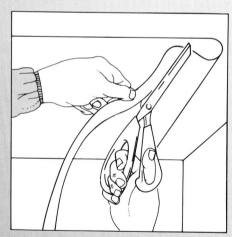

6 Trim 3mm (⅛in) outside the crease so you get a slight turn of paper on to the wall. Press the paper back in

place. Hang the second piece in the same way, matching it this time to the edge of the first length, ensuring that the pattern matches correctly.

PENDANT LIGHT FITTING

If you have a central pendant light (or ceiling rose), cut the paper to length, then measure the position of the light and mark it on the back of the paper. Allow for trimming. Paste the paper, then make a series of star-shaped cuts from the centre of the light position.

1 Hang the paper in the normal way, then when you reach the light fitting, feed the pendant through the hole and press the paper in place around the fitting.

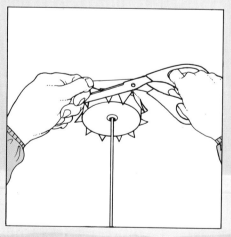

2 Crease each flap with the blunt edge of your scissors, then carefully cut off the surplus paper 3mm (⅛in) outside the score marks. Press the

paper in place, and wipe any surplus paste from the fitting with a clean cloth.

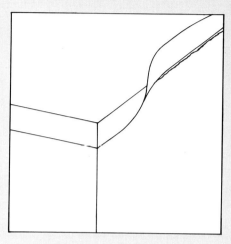

Crack between wall and ceiling
Where there is a slight crack and you do not wish to use a coving, allow about 5mm (¼in) on all your lengths to cover the crack completely. There is no filler strong enough to resist slight movement at this point.

READY-PASTED PAPER

Before following the step-by-steps, right, you will need a starting point for the first length of paper. Measure out 48cm (19in) from the window wall corner and make a pencil mark at just below picture rail level. Extend your plumb line cord and let the line hang down to just above skirting board level. Have someone standing by to make marks on the wall immediately behind the line.

Check the distance between each mark and the corner. If the wall is out of true and the reading is more than 48cm (19in) at any point, move your plumb line nearer to the wall and make a new set of marks. Make sure that you get a good turn of paper on to the window wall.

Ready-pasted paper will not stretch, so there is less chance of bubbling through expansion.

Before soaking, check for manufacturer's instructions and follow them, if different.

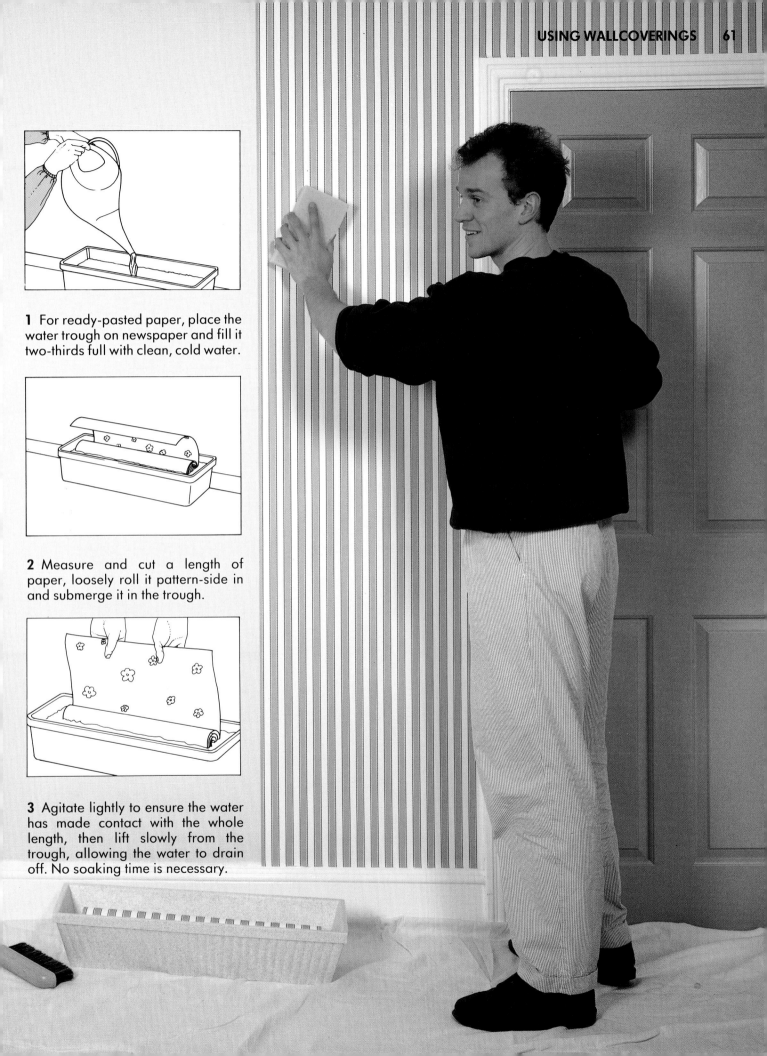

1 For ready-pasted paper, place the water trough on newspaper and fill it two-thirds full with clean, cold water.

2 Measure and cut a length of paper, loosely roll it pattern-side in and submerge it in the trough.

3 Agitate lightly to ensure the water has made contact with the whole length, then lift slowly from the trough, allowing the water to drain off. No soaking time is necessary.

PAPERING WALLS

If you are mixing your own paste, be sure to add the powder to the water in small quantities so it can be absorbed without lumping. Allow the paste time to develop before you start using it.

Do not use lumpy paste. Work the paste through a fine sieve with a wooden spoon. Be sure to wash the sieve and the spoon well if the paste contains fungicide. Cover paste at night to prevent it from drying out.

1 Make sure the pasting table is dry and clean, then, if you are right handed, lay the bottom of the paper on the table pattern-side down and with the surplus to your left, lightly rolled. If you are left handed, put the spare paper to your right.

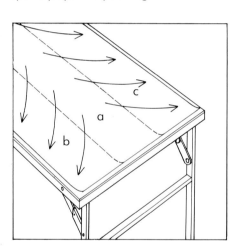

2 Load the brush with paste and apply a strip down the centre of the paper (a) on to the table. Reload the brush and work out from the centre,

herring-bone fashion (b and c), lifting the brush off as you reach the edge of the paper. Check that edges are covered with paste.

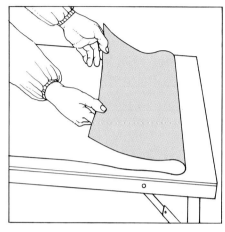

3 Carefully fold the pasted paper back on itself, lift the paper from the table and ask a helper to wipe any paste from the table with a damp cloth. Lower the paper to the table, then slide it to your right, bringing the unpasted surplus paper on to the table. Usually you only have to do this once. Reload the brush and apply paste as before. Check the edges and ends for paste.

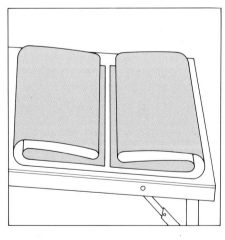

4 Fold the paper in on itself so it almost meets the other fold. The last fold will be the top of the piece. Fold it again to make the length easy to move, and place it out of the way to soak. This is most important as the paper will continue to expand for some minutes. If you fail to let it

---

USING NOVAMURA

If you choose Novamura for your wallcovering, remember that the technique for applying it is different. Cut it as for normal wallpaper, but then apply paste to the wall. Offer the length of wallcovering to the adhesive and smooth it into place.

The best tool for smoothing is a foam paint roller. It applies firm, even pressure without marking the surface.

Trim as for normal paper and wipe surplus paste from the woodwork before it dries.

---

expand fully you may get bubbles.

While the paper is soaking, paste one or two more pieces and place in order of pasting. Wipe the pasting table with a damp cloth and move your stool or steps in place, ready to hang the first length.

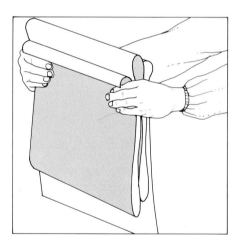

5 Carry the first pasted length to the wall as shown above.
6 Unfold the top fold and let the paper drop. At this stage it is an advantage to have a helper to control the bottom of the paper. Offer the left-hand edge of the paper to your pencilled line, ensuring that you have about 5cm (2in) spare at the top for trimming. Once the left edge is correctly positioned, wipe your hand across to the right to secure the top of the paper to the wall. Keep the paper in place while your helper

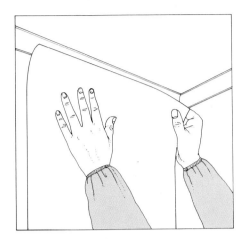

releases the bottom fold and lets the paper drop free.

7 With the paper in the correct position, take the smoothing brush and run it down the centre of the length, pressing the paper lightly to the wall. Now use the brush in light, outward strokes until the length is in place.

About 25mm (1in) of paper should have turned on to the window wall, so lightly press this in place, ensuring that there are no wrinkles in the paper. (See also page 64, Step 10.)

Do not force the paper down at the skirting and picture rail in the corner, as you will have to cut the paper here when you trim. If the turned edge seems dry, apply a little extra paste with the pasting brush.

Before trimming, smooth the paper again from the centre out, making sure the edges are stuck down. You may need to use a clean, dry cloth to dab edges down. Avoid a rubbing action, as this can cause shiny patches on some papers.

Lightly dab any bubbles flat, then leave the paper to dry. Usually they will disappear as the paper tightens.

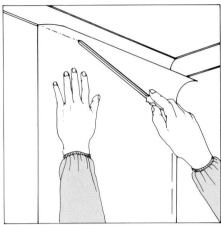

8 Use the edge of your closed scissors to press the paper firmly into the top edge, skirting board and picture rail. Run the edge of the scissors across the full width of the wallpaper. If your scissor edges are so sharp that they will score the wallcovering, use a thumb nail or more blunt edge instead. Press very lightly or you will tear the damp paper.

HANGING SPECIAL WALLCOVERINGS

If you decide to use an unusual wallcovering such as hessian, silk, cork or foil, use the recommended paste. Check as well whether the paste should be applied to the walls or to the back of the material. For example, with paper-backed hessian you paste the backing, but with unbacked hessian you paste the wall.

Roll sizes may also differ from standard wallcoverings. If so, adjust the number you buy.

Most special coverings cannot be matched at the edges, so plan to overlap the seams by about 1cm (⅓in) then use a straight-edge and knife to cut through both layers. Remove the surplus paper and the seams should match perfectly.

TAKING OUT CREASES

Sometimes, when a wall is out of true, the paper may crease when pressed into position because there is nowhere for the surplus paper to go. In this case, lift the paper from the wall and tear it along the line of the crease.

If you look carefully you will see that one edge of the torn paper on the wall shows white while the other shows only pattern. Lay the patterned flap over the visible white edge, then brush out the top patterned paper over the tear until smooth. Because the edge of the paper is chamfered by the tear, the join will be virtually invisible when it dries out.

Do not use scissors to cut the crease. A hard cut edge will always be visible.

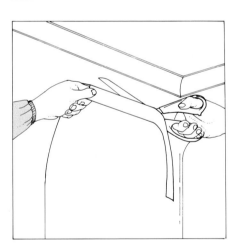

9 Wallpapers are best trimmed with scissors, as the damp paper tends to tear very easily when a knife is used. Pull the paper away from the wall just far enough to enable you to get the scissors in position, then cut about 3mm (⅛in) outside the score mark.

If there is an ugly join between wall and rail, leave about 3mm (⅛in) outside the score mark so the paper just turns on to the rail. With the surplus removed, carefully dab the paper back in place. Repeat the process at the dado rail and/or at the skirting end of the length.

Vinyls and heavy papers can be trimmed with a knife and a steel straightedge. Once the paper has been creased, position the straight-edge just a fraction above the crease and cut with the knife. Be sure to use a sharp knife or the paper will tear — a snap-off blade is ideal, for the cutting edge will blunt quite quickly as it comes into contact with the plaster. The alternative is to use a metal cutting guide, which you position under the edge of the paper.

10 When you have finished the first piece, check the edges of the paper to see that they are well stuck down. With the lighter wallcoverings this is usually no problem, but you may find some heavier papers curl slightly. Try dabbing them down with a clean, dry rag, but if the paste has dried, smear a little extra under the edge of the paper with the paste brush. Wipe away the surplus, then dab down.

If the paper has a well defined texture, be careful how you do this. If the texture is hollow behind, pressing down will flatten the relief and it will not recover. In this case you will have to accept that part of the pattern may be raised away from the wall. However, if you are working with a blown vinyl wallcovering, the foamed texture will recover fully if it is flattened as its backing is smooth.

Problems are most often encountered with smooth vinyls, where the edges frequently seem to curl away from the wall. Instead of applying more paste, use a special seam adhesive, which is supplied in a small tube. Apply it sparingly under the edge, then press the edge in place. It is possible to use a clear resin adhesive, but you must take care not to get it on the surface of the vinyl as the adhesive will soften it.

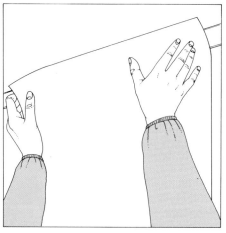

11 With the second length pasted, folded and soaked, carry it to the wall, drop out the top fold and offer the right hand corner to the wall (assuming you are working from right to left), lining it up with the edge of the first length. Match any pattern by sliding the paper up and down slightly, then ask a helper to release the second fold and align the paper edge with the edge of the first piece. Then smooth the top of the paper to the wall. Run the smoothing brush down the length of the paper and brush out towards the first length. Check that the seams align perfectly, then continue adding lengths.

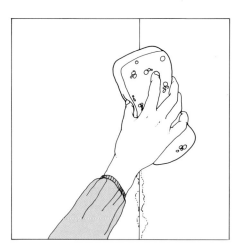

12 As you progress, clean up between each length. Use a damp cloth or sponge to wipe paste from picture rails, skirtings and window and door frames while it is still soft. Pick up trimmed pieces of paper and keep pieces for patching. Wipe the pasting table between lengths. Change trough water occasionally.

BLISTERING

Paper bubbling from the wall is mainly caused by allowing insufficient time for pasted paper to expand before it is applied to the wall. Alternatively it may be due to the poor adhesion of a lining or backing paper. The new paste swells the poorly stuck paper and it expands and bubbles. Very often it will shrink back, but this can take some time, so do not be too hasty in taking remedial action.

Waft the wall with a hair dryer to speed up drying in cold weather. If the bubbles fail to dry out, and there are not too many, cut a cross on a bubble with a razor blade, carefully lift the four flaps and apply adhesive with an artists' camel hair brush. Dab the paper back in place. If the result is satisfactory, treat the other blisters.

Where blistering is severe, you will need to strip off the length and repaper. Allow plenty of time for the new length to soak.

PAPERING AWKWARD AREAS

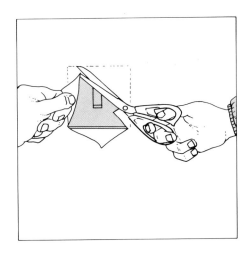

Wall-mounted light switch To paper around a raised switch, first drape the pasted length of paper over it. Feel for the centre and press to mark the paper. Now make star cuts in the paper out from the centre of the switch to the edge, then finish hanging the length.

Press the cut paper tightly around the switch and mark it with the scissors. Pull each flap away and trim it to overlap about 2mm (1⁄16in). Dab the pieces back. Wipe the paste from the switch.

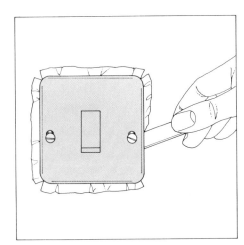

Flush-mounted switch Cut off the supply to that circuit, loosen the screws and ease the plate away from the wall. Drape the paper over the switch, find the centre, and make two diagonal cuts out to the plate corners. Trim the paper 5mm (1⁄4in) inside the switch area, then tuck it in behind the switch plate. Retighten the screws and wipe away paste.

PAPERING A RECESS

When you reach a recess, offer the unpasted length which will turn into the recess to the wall, and mark the area of surplus paper. You need enough for the depth of the recess plus about 25mm (1in) for trimming. You need to continue a strip above the recess, plus about 25mm (1in) to turn on to the ceiling of the recess. Cut away surplus paper. If the paper will not reach the full depth of the recess, cut it so that 25mm (1in) turns the corner and add a further panel of paper later.

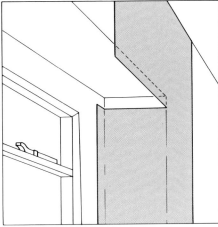

1 Make a horizontal cut at the window ledge and then at the top edge, leaving a 25mm (1in) overhang. Turn the side panel into the recess wall and smooth. Crease and trim surplus.

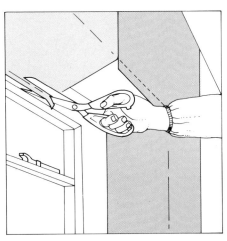

2 Paste and hang your next length of paper, allowing sufficient to reach the full depth of the ceiling recess,

plus 25mm (1in) for trimming. Crease and trim with scissors.

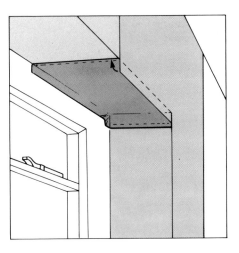

3 Now cut a panel to finish the recess ceiling. Test it for size, remembering to add 25mm (1in) for trimming at the window and recess walls. Paste, and bring the front edge of the ceiling panel to meet the front edge of the recess. Smooth on to the ceiling, crease and trim away surplus paper at window and recess walls. Cut into the corner of the overhanging paper; fold it back onto the ceiling panel for a neat edge.

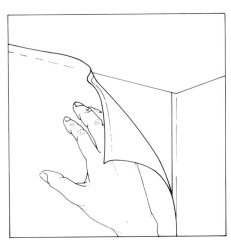

Internal corners Here the overlap can be taken right into the corner. The slight mismatch of pattern should not be noticeable there.

With thick materials where an overlap would show, use a sharp knife and straightedge to cut through both thicknesses of the overlap and remove the waste pieces.

PAPERING AN ARCHWAY

Papering an archway is not a difficult operation – but it calls for careful trimming. When you reach the arch, hold up your next length of paper, and mark on the back of the paper the necessary curve. Measure out from the pencil line a distance of 25mm (1in) and cut to this line. You now have 25mm (1in) surplus paper which will turn into the archway.

1 Now cut V-shaped notches along the strip to be turned, as illustrated, then hang the paper in the normal way. Press the tabs down, ensuring they lie flat, as they will be covered by paper later.

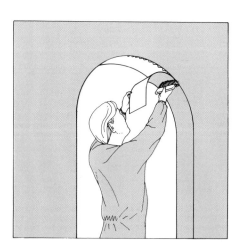

2 When you have completed the archway, measure the depth of the arch and cut two lengths of paper which meet at the centre of the arch curve with a slight overlap. Paste and hang, pressing edges down.

PAPERING ROUND A DOOR

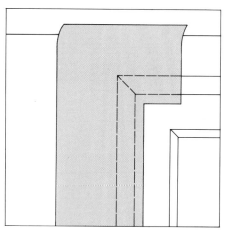

1 Cut the length of paper that will be fitted round the door, marking the spare 50mm (2in) allowed for trimming top and bottom on the back of the paper. Measure the distance from the edge of the last hung length to the door frame and add 25mm (1in). Do this near the top of the door and at the base and mark these distances on the prepared length of paper. Draw a line between them.

Measure the height from the skirting to the top of the door frame and deduct 25mm (1in). Mark this point on your drawn line. Draw a horizontal line from it to the doorway side. Cut out the surplus.

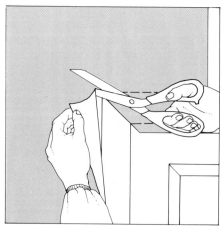

2 Hang the length as normal, running it over the top of the door and pressing it into the frame. You need to make a diagonal cut at the frame corner to allow the surplus paper to be pressed down.

3 With the paper smoothed down, use closed scissors or a stiff brush edge to score a crease around the door frame.

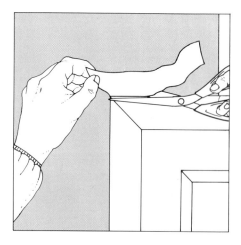

4 Pull the paper away from the wall and trim with scissors, or, if you are working with heavy paper or vinyl, use the straightedge and knife. (*See page 64, Vinyls and Heavy Papers.*)

Now work from the other side of the door, and cut your length in the same way if the two pieces will meet above the door frame. Even so, it is wise to drop a plumb line to the right-hand edge of this length, so you hang the piece vertically.

If the two pieces will not meet you will need an infill piece. If you want to continue the pattern match this should be cut and hung before the next full length is cut.

If matching is no problem, you could hang the next full length first, then cut the infill piece.

PAPERING ROUND A LAVATORY

In most cases, unless an obstacle involves a large area of paper, leave trimming until the paper is on the wall. Take your time, and have scissors at hand to make cuts.

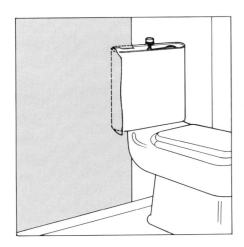

1 To paper around a low-flush lavatory, first remove the lid from the cistern. Take the paper close to the cistern, then make a diagonal cut towards the corner of it so you can tuck the paper against the cistern horizontally and vertically. Trim on the generous side and tuck the surplus behind the cistern, dabbing it in place with a smoothing brush.

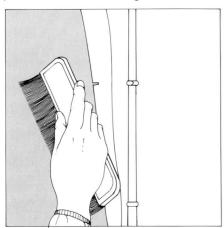

2 If there is a soil pipe, make a vertical cut to allow the paper to pass around the pipe, then make star-shaped cuts (*see page 60, Pendant Light Fitting*), trimming off surplus paper. Where possible, tuck paper down behind small pipes. Make cuts to allow for pipe clips.

PAPERING BEHIND RADIATORS

If you have a modern central heating system with steel radiators, it may be possible to swing the radiators away from the walls so you can paper behind them — it depends upon whether the installer allowed enough pipe when he or she connected the system. Try lifting a radiator. If it rises enough to clear the holding brackets, you can slightly loosen the pipe nuts either side of the radiator and lean it forward.

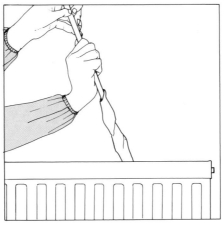

If the radiator will not move — and this will certainly apply with older systems — you will have to tuck the paper down behind it. Cut two slits where the holding brackets are located. Use a small radiator roller, or improvise with a length of wood or broom handle wrapped in clean rag, to smooth the paper down.

BLOCKING OFF A FIREPLACE
If you plan to block off a fireplace which is not used regularly, be sure to use a fire-resistant board. Non-combustible boards which contain no asbestos are available. You must insert a small ventilator in the panel so that air still circulates in the flue. This will reduce the risk of damp through condensation on the flue lining. The board can be decorated with wallpaper to match the room.

PAPERING ROUND A FIREPLACE

If your fireplace is a feature of the room — and if it is on a chimney breast — it is best to hang a length of paper centrally, then paper out in each direction. Any slight discrepancy in the pattern run can be lost round the internal corners of the chimney breast.

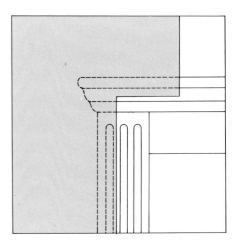

1 At the sides of the surround, cut the paper as if you were tackling a door frame. You will also have to make cuts in the paper to let the mantelpiece come through. Allow extra paper to push into mouldings.

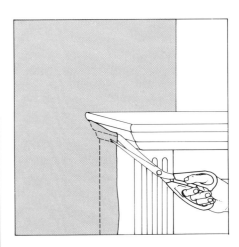

2 Trim along crease marks with scissors. With odd shapes, such as the shape made by a stone fireplace, make small cuts in the paper edge, mould it to the required contours and crease. Trim 3 mm (⅛ in) outside the crease line so the paper just turns on to the stone.

DECORATIVE IDEAS

Interesting wallcovering motifs can be cut out and used on furniture, doors and items like waste bins. Vinyls or washables can be wiped clean, or use ordinary wallpaper motifs sprayed with an artist's clear protective varnish. You can buy this from artists' suppliers.

Fixing motifs

Cut out your motifs with small scissors and apply wallpaper paste; allow soaking time, then place into position and dab lightly to remove bubbles. Wipe away any surplus with a damp cloth.

To reduce the impact of plain doors you could add complete panels of matching wallpaper.

Friezes, so fashionable in the 1930s, can be used to add an extra touch of colour and pattern. They can be run around door and window frames or under picture rails. Ideally the colouring should blend with the wallcovering rather than form a strong contrast.

There are a number of friezes available which have been especially designed for applying along Gyproc coving, adding both colour and extra texture to the surface.

Stencils for friezes

A whole range of pre-cut stencils is available which can be used again and again. Special paints in crayon-form ensure no drips or smudges. Paint is stippled on with a special stencil brush. Stencils are effective on textured surfaces as well as smooth. As stencil sheets are flexible, they can also be used on items like lampshades.

Below: Parachutists provide unusual decoration for the walls of this attic room. Stencilled in a soft brown, they pick out the warm tones of the natural wood floorboards

Above: A stencilled border of roses and leaves is echoed in the lighter design on lower walls

Left: Trompe l'œil terracotta pots of colourful flowering plants provide a focal point

Below: Wallpaper borders can be used at dado, picture rail or skirting level

TILING

Tiling is a very simple job, in that tiles come in easy-to-handle units and the work can be done over any period. The first task is to decide what area you wish to cover. In kitchens and bathrooms which have been papered, it is wise to install tile splash-backs around sinks and basins. In the bedroom, a tiled area round a vanity unit is practical as well as decorative.

You may wish to do half-tiling. If an area is already tiled, you may apply the new tiles over the old providing they are firmly stuck to the wall and the surface is smooth and flat. Choose tiles to complement existing fittings, kitchen units and so on. (*See also pages 8-13.*)

Full floor-to-ceiling tiling is probably the most attractive style for the bathroom, but it can prove quite an expense in a large room. (*See also page 35.*)

It is important that the walls are in good condition, so spend time preparing them. Any irregularities in the surface will be accentuated by the reflection in glazed tiles.

Surfaces for tiling

It is not wise to tile on to plain brickwork, even though special thick bed tile adhesives are available. If you have stripped away old plaster it is best to apply new plaster and allow it to dry before tiling.

Never be tempted to tile over wallpaper, however firmly stuck. Remember that tiles are heavy in quantity, and all that will be holding them to the wall is wallpaper paste. Strip back to bare plaster.

You can tile over painted walls provided the paint is firmly adhered and not flaking or peeling away. Rub high gloss paint with medium-to-coarse damp abrasive paper or a flexible sanding pad to afford a better grip for adhesive. No prepara-tion is necessary for tiling over old tiles, as modern adhesives will grip firmly to the glazed surface.

You can also tile direct on to plasterboard, plywood (preferably of the WBP grade, which is moisture-resistant) and oil-tempered hardboard which is held firmly in place so the surface is flat.

Remember that areas near baths, basins and showers should be tiled using water-resistant adhesive and grout. Seal the gaps where the tiles meet the bath, basin or shower tray with a flexible sealant.

CEILING TILES

Ceiling tiles can be very useful to disguise a poor ceiling surface or add insulation to a cold ceiling.

Expanded polystyrene tiles are the most common for domestic use, and they are usually 300mm (12in) or 600mm (24in) square with chamfered edges. They should be fixed with special tile adhesive, and this must be spread over the whole ceiling. Do not use the old 'five blob' method of fixing as in a fire tiles melt away from the glue, causing them to drop from the ceiling. Modern tiles are all self extinguishing grade (SX) so they are no great fire risk, even though the plastic melts.

To calculate how many tiles you need, divide the squared area of one tile into the squared ceiling area.

It is best to find the centre of a room, as with floor tiling, and tile out from a centre point. However, if there is a true, straight wall at the entrance to the room you could start there and work away. Trim the tiles with a craft knife and straightedge.

Fibrous tiles and gypsum plaster tiles are also available for ceiling work, but as they are much heavier they must be pinned to battens screwed to the ceiling. Find out which way the ceiling joists run and fix the battens at right angles, spaced so that the ceiling tiles will

Ceiling tiles can be used to disguise a poor surface, but need to be well secured

meet at their centres. Battens of 30mm × 15mm (1¼in × ½in) are adequate for most tiles, screwed into each joist for the run of the batten. If the tiles are tongued and grooved, no cross-pieces are necessary, but with some square-edge tiles it may be advisable to fit cross-pieces between the battens to give support on all

edges. Pin the tiles through the edges, or use special clips which are hidden by the adjoining tiles.

If you wish to paint your tiles, the ideal time to do this is before you put them up. Use either emulsion or a fire-retardant paint – never gloss paint as this can assist the spread of flames should there be a fire.

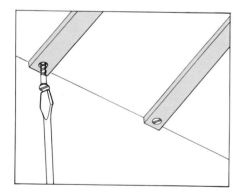

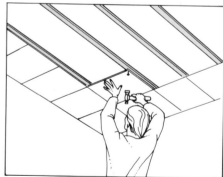

1 Locate the ceiling joists with a joist-finding tool, and mark the ceiling. Mark the spacing of the battens in relation to the width of the tiles. Cut the battens to length, and drill and countersink them: screws must penetrate 25mm (1in) into the joist. Screw in place.

2 Use a roller to paint the faces of the tiles, then paint chamfered edges with a narrow brush. You may need two coats to give sufficient depth of colour. Gypsum tiles may be fissured. These may be left unpainted, or you can use a brush to stipple paint into the textured surface.

3 Follow the fixing directions supplied with your tiles. Pin through the edges, angling the pins and sinking the pin heads into the edges. With tongued and grooved tiles, pin through the tongue or use special holding clips which grip the tile and are then pinned to the batten.

TILING WALLS

Calculate the number of tiles you will need. (*See page 36*.) Deduct from this total any patterned tiles or tile sets you plan to incorporate in the tiling and allow a few extra tiles in case of breakage. It may be difficult to order just a few extra tiles later on.

Checking the tiles

Check the batch numbers on the boxes and try to ensure all numbers are the same: tiles from different batches may vary slightly in colour. Even with boxes of the same batch number it is wise to mix them so that any variations are lost.

When ordering tiles, remember items such as towel rails, toilet roll holders, soap dishes and hooks. Some are incorporated in the tiles.

Check that the tiles have some finished edges. Universal tiles are mixed and include edge tiles. A few ranges require special edging tiles.

From your tile total, calculate how much adhesive and grout you need — you may prefer to use a combined adhesive and grout. You should get a spreader with the adhesive.

Starting work

To help you position your tiles, select a long, straight batten (gauge stick), and mark tile widths on it, including the gap for grouting. (*See below*.) Then tape tile-sized paper

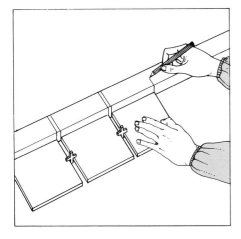

squares on the walls to represent where you want your patterned tiles. Always position them at least one tile in from corners.

Mark out a rough tile grid on the wall, starting on the window wall. Use your gauge stick to get the right balance horizontally, then use the stick vertically to ensure you will get a full tile at the window sill. You need tiled areas to be well balanced. Avoid having thin slivers of tile or cut tiles where they will show. If you need to do any tile cutting at floor level, make a pencil mark to indicate the base of the first full tile above floor level. Never tile up from the floor. It could be uneven and throw all your tiling out.

1 Take the tiles from a number of boxes and mix them, then lay out a row on the floor, positioning them to the marks you have made on the walls. Check for balance either side of the window. Look at any pattern on the tiles. Is it really random, or is there a motif which suggests the tiles should go a certain way up?

Mark the positions of towel rail and toilet roll holder tiles, if you are using them, before you start tiling.

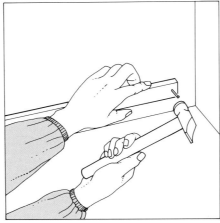

2 Starting on your window wall, look for the pencil mark representing the first full tile above floor level, and position a batten at this level. Ask someone to hold the batten while you check it is horizontal with a spirit level. Then secure it to the wall by lightly tapping in masonry nails. Position a vertical batten to the outer edge of the first row of full tiles from the corner. Check the batten is vertical with a spirit level and secure.

3 Starting at the batten, apply tile adhesive to the wall with the notched spreader, covering about 1 sq m (yd) at a time. The spreader should leave a layer about 3mm (⅛in) thick. Lift away any surplus adhesive.

If you find it easier, apply adhesive to the wall with a small trowel, then merely use the notched spreader to get the correct thickness.

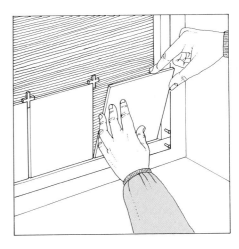

4 Place your first tile against the wall on the inside corner of the battens, pressing it firmly in place. Try not to slide tiles as this forces adhesive up on to the tile edge.

With the first tile in place, insert a cross-shaped spacer (*see page 35*) at the top corner and position your next tile alongside the first so that it sits tightly against the spacer.

Continue tiling until the horizontal run is complete. You can leave cut tiles until later, completing all full tiling in a wall area first.

CUTTING TILES

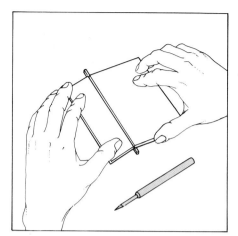

the arm, or by applying downward pressure on the arm, depending upon the type of cutter you are using.

Very thin sections of tile may have to be removed after scoring by snapping away the waste with pincers. Any rough edges that remain after doing this can be rubbed away with a tile file, which is designed especially for this job.

A wheel cutter which is hand-held can be used to cut tiles with a reasonably soft body or use a tungsten carbide-tipped stylus. Mark the tile on the glazed side with a chinagraph pencil and run the cutter along the line against a steel rule, pressing just hard enough for you to hear the cutter whisper across the glaze. Only make one pass of the cutter. Place matchsticks under the score line and press either side of it to snap the tile.

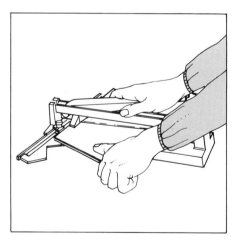

A platform cutter should be used for modern tiles which are too hard for wheel cutters to be used. Set the gauge to the width of tile to be cut; position the tile on the platform and, holding the arm of the cutter, use it to push the cutting wheel across the tile. Exert just enough pressure so that you can hear the wheel whisper over the glaze, leaving a score mark.

The tile may then be snapped either between the jaws at the end of

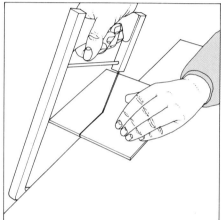

A tile saw Cutting around obstructions has always been the most difficult operation when tiling, and the traditional way of tackling the problem is to mark the tile on the glazed face, score by hand with a tile cutter, then nibble away waste with pliers or pincers. However, a tile saw simplifies the operation and makes the risk of breakage far less likely.

The saw consists of a circular cutting blade tipped with granules of tungsten carbide, held in a large metal frame. The blade cuts in any direction, and the size of the frame enables you to turn the saw around a tile without obstruction.

Mark the area to be removed on the face of the tile, then use the saw to cut it away.

The blade will eventually blunt – its life will depend upon the hardness of the tiles being shaped – but you can easily buy replacement blades.

A word of caution. Never mark tiles on the reverse side with a felt tip pen. The ink can soak through the body of the tile, appearing as a stain under the glaze where it cannot be reached.

Nibble with pincers If you decide to nibble with pincers, mark the area to be cut away, then support the main part of the tile on a flat surface with the area to be shaped overhanging. Hold the tile firmly and start nibbling away from the tile edge, slowly working to the score line and only taking small pieces away.

If a pipe has to pass through a tile, mark the hole position then cut the tile in two, with the cut passing through the centre of the hole. Nibble away the waste from each tile.

A template former or profile gauge is a helpful tool for awkward shapes. This consists of a number of needles or strips of plastic which are held in a frame but slide freely. When pressed against a shaped surface, the tool takes up the exact shape, which can then be transferred to a tile by following the outline with a chinagraph pencil (never a felt-tip pen).

GROUTING

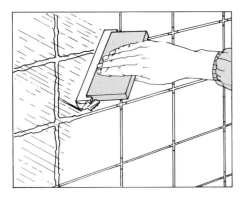

1 If the grout is in powder form, mix it to a thick paste as recommended by the manufacturer. Grout from a tub is ready-mixed. Force the grout into the gaps between the tiles, making sure no holes are left.

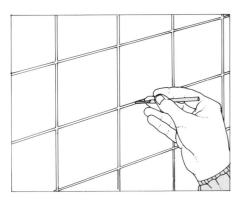

2 Wipe away surplus from the tile surface, then smooth the grout with an item such as a ball point pen top or a special grouting tool (supplied with tiling kits for this purpose).

3 Allow the grout to dry, then rub the surface of the tile with a tightly-rolled ball of newspaper. This removes surplus grout and polishes the tiles at the same time.

DRILLING

The main problem with drilling tiles is getting through the glaze without the drill tip skating over the shiny surface. Use a sharp masonry bit and, if you have a power drill with variable speed, set it so that the drill is just rotating. This way you have full control over it. Never use a power drill set to hammer action – the vibration will shatter them.

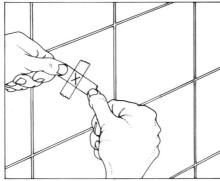

1 Mark the spot to be drilled with a chinagraph pencil, then apply two strips of clear adhesive tape over the spot to form a cross. This will help to hold the drill tip in place until the glaze has been cut.

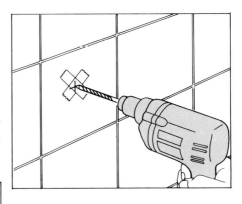

2 Apply only gentle pressure while drilling to avoid damaging the tile.

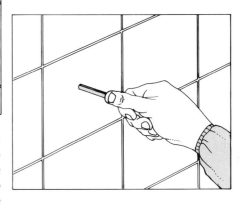

3 Push wall plugs into the drilled holes and use screws which match the plugs for size. Never force in a screw or you may crack the tile.

Choose from a wide range of bathroom fittings and accessories which are both decorative and functional. Some are inset in tiles. **Clockwise from top:** *Towel rail, toothbrush and mug holder, towel ring, shell soap dish, soap tray (above), tile and edging tiles (below and left), toilet roll holder, sponges*

TILING A SPLASHBACK AND SHOWER

If you have never tackled tiling, a splashback is an easy way to start as it involves only a small area. Check that the back of the sink or basin is horizontal. If it is true, tiling can follow this line.

With a freestanding basin, it is wise to extend the tiling by one tile either side. Place a steel rule across the back of the basin and make a pencil line on the wall where the extended tiles will sit. Pin a piece of hardboard to this line so they will have something to rest on while the adhesive sets.

Use water-resistant adhesive to fix the tiles, then a waterproof grout to seal the gaps.

If the wall is papered, it is best to apply adhesive to the back of the tiles which overlap the paper, within 3mm (⅛in) of the edges, rather than risk getting adhesive on the paper. If this does happen, wipe off the adhesive while it is still wet.

Tiling a shower cabinet

In most situations a shower enclosure will involve two walls of the room, but should a third wall need to be constructed, use marine plywood on a framework of pretreated timber. The plywood will be unaffected by damp. Make sure you use both waterproof adhesive and grout. The technique for tiling is the same as for the rest of the room.

The most vital factor with a shower enclosure is to ensure that all gaps are carefully sealed. Pay particular attention where tiles meet the shower tray. The tray must be firm and not flex in any way, and meeting edges must be dry before you apply sealant.

Use a silicone rubber sealant, either clear or in a colour to match the tray as closely as possible. Leave the sealant to set before you use the shower. Follow the manufacturer's instructions.

Sealing gaps

Gap sealing is also important behind basins, sinks and baths. Use a silicone rubber sealant or a plastic sealing strip stuck in place either

with the adhesive supplied or with a clear silicone rubber sealant. Some are self-adhesive. Ceramic quadrants, or edging tiles, may be available in matching tile colours. You can stick these to the wall with waterproof tile adhesive and seal them to the bath or basin with silicone rubber sealant.

Above: When tiling around baths, basins, and so on, use water-resistant materials
Below: The small size of mosaic tiles means that less cutting is necessary

APPLYING SEALANT

Applying sealant to a gap can be a sticky business, and it is a good idea to practise first. Some dispensers have winged applicators which help shape the sealant as it leaves the cartridge, but with a straight nozzle, the simplest way to get a neat result is to run a strip of masking tape either side of the area to be sealed. Run the sealant between the tape, then, while it is still soft, wet your finger and run it quickly along the sealant, pressing it home and shaping it. Then immediately pull away the masking tape, leaving a neat line of sealant. If some sealant should get smeared in the wrong place and it starts to set, leave it until cured, then cut and peel it away with a razor blade.

TILING A WORKTOP

Tiles used for a worktop must be far tougher than those normally used on the wall, so do not be tempted to use up wall tiles for this job. Choose tiles recommended for worktops, or flooring-grade ones, well able to withstand knocks. You can buy sheets of mosaic tiles, sold ready-spaced, mounted on to netting.

As the tiles are tougher, you may find your existing tile cutter cannot cope, in which case it will pay to borrow an industrial cutter from your local hire shop. This will cope with tiles of 10mm (¼in) thickness and upward.

Try to plan your worktop so that you can use multiples of tiles without the need for cutting. This will look neater and may even obviate cutting altogether. Shaping can be a problem, for while the tile saw will cut hard tiles, its blade will blunt quite quickly.

Some worktop tiles have matching edging strips to give a neat, rounded appearance to tiling. For many kinds, however, you will need to produce an edging, and this can be done using plastic trim strips designed to sandwich under the row of edge tiles as they are laid.

Always use waterproof adhesive, and space the tiles with slightly larger X spacers (*see page 35*) produced for floor tiles. Finish with a waterproof grout, and seal the joint between worktop and wall with a silicone rubber sealant or with a plastic edging strip. Some of the latter may need sticking in place with the adhesive supplied, while others are self-adhesive.

Tiling over old tiles

If you have a room where old tiles are firmly bedded to the wall, removing them could be a major task – often resulting in the walls needing replastering, particularly in old homes where tiles were originally set in cement mortar. In this case, provided the tiles are firmly bedded and the wall is flat, leave the tiles on and tile over them. Make sure tiles are clean and grease-free, and lay out new tiles so that the joints of the old and new tiles do not align. With modern tile adhesives there is no problem with bonding.

You need to start one tile up from the floor, working to a horizontal batten. To save drilling into the old tiles you can use double-sided adhesive pads to hold the batten in place. Use plenty of pads so the batten can resist the weight of the new tiles.

If the walls were previously half-tiled, you will now end up with a thicker ledge where your tiling finishes. Finish with edging tiles or make a feature of the step by bonding a hardwood strip along the top. Gloss paint or varnish the strip first to make it water resistant. Provide a smooth top using a plaster repair filler, then, when this has set, bond the wood to it using a PVA wood adhesive. When fixing towel rails and so on, use plugs and screws long enough to reach into the wall plaster – old tiles will not support the weight of fittings.

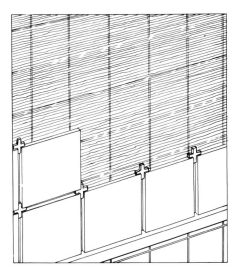
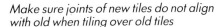

Make sure joints of new tiles do not align with old when tiling over old tiles

Finish the thick double edge of a twice half-tiled wall with edging tiles

FLOORING

Your choice of floorcovering may be governed by how much money you are prepared to spend. Floorboards which are in good condition can be stained and sealed and, with the addition of slip mats and rugs, can be an attractive and inexpensive alternative to carpeting. You may prefer the practicality of carpet squares or choose warm close-carpeting with a good quality underlay.

In an area such as a hall you should take into account the durability of floorcoverings. This applies to the kitchen, too—there are carpets suitable for kitchen use, but a cushioned vinyl may prove easier to keep clean. Carpet is luxurious in the bathroom, or you may prefer cork tiles or sheet vinyl. Whichever type of floorcovering you choose, careful preparation of the floor is essential.

PREPARING THE FLOOR

It is essential that any floor to be covered is clean, dry and smooth. Smoothness is important, for any projections left on the floor will quickly ruin a covering.

Solid floors

If a floor shows signs of dampness, it is important to deal with it. Covering it up could make matters worse. If the trouble is caused by moisture condensing on a cold surface, this usually clears up when the floor-covering is laid.

If the floor is smooth but dusty, vacuum off the dust, then treat the floor with a coat of PVA adhesive, diluted one part adhesive to four parts clean water. This will seal the surface and prevent further dust arising.

If the floor has projecting nibs of concrete, remove these with a steel chisel or bolster and club hammer. If the floor is uneven, it is best to use a screeding compound to level it. You can buy this either as a powder which you mix with water, or ready-mixed in a tub.

Clean the floor thoroughly then use a little of the compound to fill holes and cracks. Allow it to set before applying the screeding compound over the whole area. It can be spread with a trowel, but the material is self-levelling, so no fine trowelling is needed.

Concrete or tiled floors Bare concrete or old quarry tiles can be painted, but make sure they are clean and dust-free first. Use a special flooring paint designed to stand up to rough wear and tear.

If the floor is dusty, seal with a solution of one part PVA adhesive to five parts water after brushing away all loose dust.

If the floor is in poor condition, coat it with a screeding compound to provide a new smooth surface. This material is self-levelling, so it is quite easy to lay.

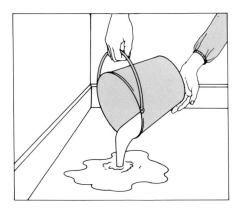

Tip screeding compound on to a floor, brush out, and leave to find its own level

The same treatment is advisable if you are dealing with slightly uneven quarry tiles. A thin screed over the whole floor will provide a much smoother surface to paint.

If you have an old property with flagstones laid on to earth, seek professional advice. Merely screeding over them to provide a level surface may not be sufficient to prevent damp rising through.

Unless traffic is light you will need to use at least two or three coats of floor paint.

Timber floors

It is just as important for a timber floor to be smooth, so examine it carefully, remove any old tacks and hammer down any raised floor nails. If the floor is uneven you have two options. The first is to lay sheet hardboard smooth-side up over the whole floor (rough-side up if you are going to use carpet tiles). This seals

any gaps and cracks between boards; but a disadvantage is that it will be difficult to get under the floor in future.

The second option is to borrow an industrial floor sander from your local hire shop and sand the floor smooth. This sander will have a dust-collecting bag, but you can still expect fine dust to escape. You may also need to hire a small belt sander to get into corners and close to walls.

Wherever possible run the sanding belt in the direction of the wood grain and always progress from coarse to fine belts.

If floorboards are in good condition, they can look attractive stained and sealed. In many cases the floor will benefit from a sanding to clean it up, whether it is uneven or not.

Dust off the floor and vacuum thoroughly after sanding and before applying any finish.

You can stain the boards in two ways. Either apply a stain or dye by brush or lint-free rag, then finish with a polyurethane seal, or use a seal which already contains a stain. The advantage of the separate stain

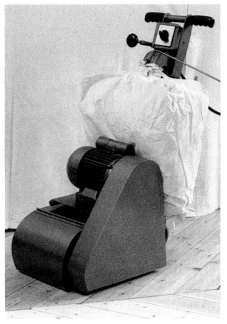

Above: *The main floor area is ideally done with a hired industrial floor sander, best suited to such large jobs*
Left: *An edging sander is necessary on floors to reach close to walls*

or dye is that however many coats of seal are applied, you will not noticeably darken the wood. With a combined stain and seal you will inevitably darken the wood further with each extra coat you apply.

It is best to test a stain on a piece of spare wood first, letting it dry thoroughly before examining the colour. Err on the lighter side if you are in any doubt.

Choose a seal which is formulated to withstand heavy wear. Some will be sold as floor seal, others will be sold as varnish.

When applying seal, work the first coat into the wood with a pad made up from an old handkerchief filled with cotton wool. This acts as a key for further coats which can be brush-applied, and it ensures that the seal does not flake away.

Chipboard flooring can also be stained and sealed, though you may find you need a few extra coats of seal to allow for the porosity of the chipboard.

Ordinary paint can be used on timber floors, but it is not a recommended finish.

CHECKING THE FLOOR

To help find small nails and tacks left in floorboards, slip an old nylon stocking over your hand and run your hand lightly over the boards. The nylon will snag on any projection it encounters. Pull out any nails and tacks you find with pincers, or, if you cannot get hold of the head of a tack, use an old chisel kept for rough jobs and lever the tack out with that.

To check if the boards are uneven, lay a straight batten across the run of the boards. Draw the curtains or turn out the lights, then shine a torch behind the batten. Light will shine under where the boards undulate.

Where the boards are badly worn, it may be possible to lift them and turn them over instead of buying new floorboards.

SHEET VINYL FLOORCOVERING

Co-ordinate your kitchen or bathroom with complementary easy-to-clean sheet vinyl

Sheet vinyl is available in strips 2 metres (6½ft) wide and in larger sheets 3 metres (10ft) or 4 metres (13ft) wide. In most cases a length of sheet will cover a floor without the necessity for joins.

As sheet vinyl is so wide, it tends to be very heavy. It is a good idea to ask someone to help you lift and position it.

If you are covering a kitchen floor, make a floor plan showing the position of doors, windows and main units. Then, having chosen your width of covering and if strips are involved, decide where best to position the first length. Always try to work at right angles to the main window, for in this way the joins will show less, and try to position the first strip so there will be no joins within the main doorway. Mark in the other lengths and, from the plan, calculate how many metres you need of the given width. You may find you have to order a few metres extra to avoid a join along a length – unless

that length could be positioned where a join would not matter. Do not forget to allow for pattern matching.

Also, wherever possible, allow for the sheet to be carried into spaces occupied by the washing machine, tumble drier or dishwasher without joins. This will ensure that, should water be spilled, there will be no

gaps for water to seep through to the floor. If there have to be joins, either for economy or convenience, bond the floorcovering to the floor, especially where the sheets meet.

Choosing the vinyl

When choosing a vinyl for kitchen use, it is best to go for a textured surface rather than a smooth one. A smooth vinyl can become slippery when wet.

You will also find there are two basic types of sheet vinyl: lay-flat, which is designed to need no fixing, and standard vinyl, which is best stuck in place with vinyl flooring adhesive. Whichever vinyl you choose, it will help with laying if you leave the vinyl in a warm room for a day or so before use. Warm plastic is more pliable than cold.

Preparation

Before you start laying, give the floor a final clean. Wash especially dirty areas with sugar soap dissolved in warm water and allow to dry. Remove whatever appliances you can, such as the washing machine and dishwasher, so that you can carry the floor covering into the gaps. One serious snag with laying vinyl up to a fitted unit is that, should the unit have to be pulled out for servicing, it may be difficult to lift it over the edge of the vinyl – especially over the thicker, cushioned types of vinyl.

CUTTING SAFELY

Sheet vinyl is not easy to cut and care is needed. Keep a sheet of scrap hardboard at hand, on which to make cuts: the knife may snag on floorboards.

Use a sharp craft knife with a snap-off blade so that you can maintain a keen edge.

Position a steel straightedge along the line of cut and use the knife so that it is always cutting away from your other hand. Do not try to get through thick vinyl in one stroke. Make a number of

passes, allowing the knife to follow the cut until it breaks through.

Where the vinyl has to be cut in situ – as when trimming to a wall – push the knife blade through the sheet, then draw it along the marked line – again making sure your holding hand is always behind the direction of cut.

Where accurate cutting is difficult, always err on the waste side of your line. It is easy to trim off a little extra, but very hard to disguise a replacement strip.

LAYING SHEET VINYL

It is best to leave your newly-bought roll of flooring loosely rolled in a warm room for 24 hours to allow it to become supple.

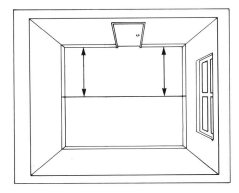

Your floor may be wider than the width of the sheet vinyl; if this is the case, mark two separate points on the floor, each mark being the width of the sheet vinyl away from the longest wall, less 5cm (2in) to allow for trimming. Draw a line between these two points with chalk, continuing the line up the skirtings.

If you need more than two sheets, ensure that the flooring is positioned correctly so that you will not be left with a thin strip of vinyl along one wall.

Cut the first length of vinyl about 5cm (2in) longer at both ends to allow for trimming. Lay the length up 5cm (2in) against the skirting on three walls.

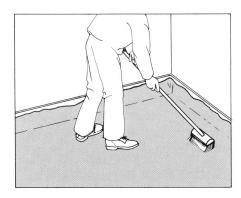

1 Sweep over the vinyl with a soft broom to ensure the sheet is in close contact with the floor. Keep one long edge of the sheet on the chalk line if you are using more than one length of the floorcovering.

LIFTING A VINYL FLOORCOVERING

If vinyl has been stuck to the floor, it can be difficult to remove. If it resists pulling away, or by doing so you are likely to damage the floor, lay a sheet of kitchen foil over the area to be lifted and apply the heat of a domestic iron until the glue is soft enough for you to pull the vinyl away from the floor. This will leave strips of adhesive behind. Soften these with heat in the same way, and remove with a flexible scraper.

An alternative is to use a hot air stripper to soften the glue, taking care not to over-do the heat. Use the heat to soften any remaining adhesive, lifting it away with a scraper.

The same principle applies with vinyl tiles. Heat the surface, then slip a scraper blade under the tile and prise it away from the floor. Heat any remaining adhesive and scrape it away.

This method is quite safe with old adhesive where the solvents will have evaporated. Do not use heat with new adhesives as solvent may remain which is a serious fire risk.

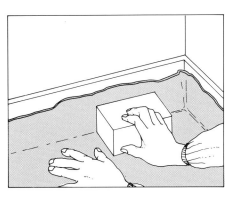

2 Use a block of wood to press the vinyl firmly into the angle between floor and skirting. You may need to make vertical release cuts into the 5cm (2in) corner flaps. You will not need to trim or use adhesive until all the fitting is complete.

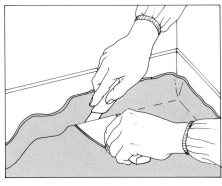

3 If a second sheet is necessary, lay it overlapping the first. Cut through both sheets and remove the

waste. Make all awkward cuts — into doorways, corners, around pedestal basins — as explained below and on the following page.

Then use a paint scraper to hold the vinyl hard against the floor where it meets the skirting, and trim off surplus with a craft knife.

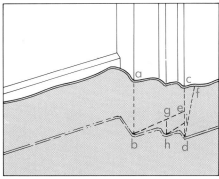

TO TRIM AROUND A DOOR FRAME

1 Make cuts in the surplus vinyl to allow the vinyl to enter the door opening.

Make two vertical 5cm (2in) cuts in the vinyl at the projecting points of the door frame, from the top of the vinyl down to the floor (**ab** and **cd**). This allows the vinyl to lie flat so you can trim it accurately.

Next make diagonal cuts to the same two points (**eb** and **fd**). Brush the vinyl so no air is trapped beneath. Make another vertical cut around the frame (**gh**) and cut diagonally (**ih**).

Press the vinyl tightly against the door frame, then trim any surplus.

2 Take the vinyl into the doorway, and trim it so that it will end halfway under the door. Finish it off later with a metal edging strip.

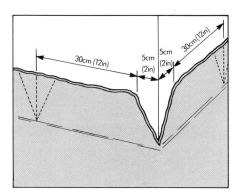

External corners. Lift the vinyl and make a vertical cut at the corner. Take the knife blade just to the floor. Make further diagonal cuts from 5cm (2in) on either side down to the base of the first cut so the vinyl will rest against each wall. Make further cuts about every 30 cm (12 in) if necessary. Hold the vinyl tight against the wall with a wood block, then position the knife with its point where wall and floor meet. Cut into the corner, holding the knife blade at an angle of 45° as you progress.

Repeat the process for the remaining flap of vinyl, making sure you get a neat fit on the corner. Again, it is better to trim away too little rather than too much: you can always pare away a little more. Finish all the fitting before sticking down the vinyl.

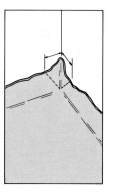 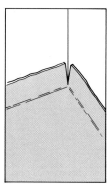

Internal corners. For areas such as in an alcove, cut all but about 25mm (1in) from the surplus vinyl running up the wall, then cut off a triangle from the corner so that when the vinyl is pressed into the corner it forms a V. This will allow you to press the vinyl to both walls so that it can be trimmed.

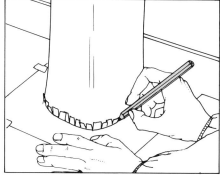

Pedestal basin. With awkward shapes it is best to make a paper template first, then transfer the shape on to the vinyl. Position your paper up against the pedestal so the amount riding up the pedestal exceeds the depth front to back. Make scissor-cuts so that you can press the paper around the pedestal base, creasing it against the base with your nail. Mark the shape with a pencil and cut away the waste paper.

With the vinyl riding up the pedestal, make a vertical cut down the vinyl at the centre point of the curve on the pedestal until it just reaches the floor. Pull the vinyl back and mark on it the shape of the pedestal base. Trim the vinyl about 6mm (¼in) within the pencil mark first, check for fit, then cut to the true mark.

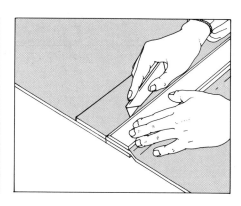

Joins. If at any point adjoining vinyl overlaps, use a straightedge and knife to cut through both thicknesses, then pull away the waste from each to give a perfect fit.

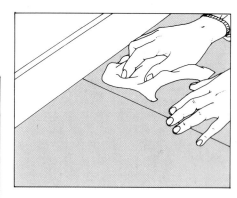

Applying adhesive. To fix down, apply flooring adhesive to the floor with a notched spreader. Check how long the adhesive should be left before the vinyl is pressed on to it. With solvent adhesives, allow plenty of ventilation and avoid smoking or any form of naked flame.

STICKING DOWN

When using lay-flat materials, it is still wise to secure the edges to prevent them being damaged by furniture or appliances being slid across them. Use either acrylic flooring adhesive along the edges, or use special double-sided adhesive carpet tape positioned evenly.

Make sure joins and any points where equipment may need to be pulled out are stuck down. Remove any excess glue at once.

LAYING VINYL TILES

Vinyl tiles are easier to handle than sheet vinyl, and simpler to cut and fit around awkward shapes – but the job will probably take a little longer. Many tile companies offer a leaflet containing a squared grid on which you can mark the size and shape of your room. From this you can calculate the number of tiles you need.

If you have no leaflet, work out the total area of floor to be covered. Then take the area of one tile and divide it into the room area to give you the number of tiles you will need. Add a few extra tiles as spares. (*See page 36, Calculating Tile Quantities.*)

If you plan to tile in alternate colours, divide your total by two and allow a few extra tiles of each colour. It is always wise to over-buy.

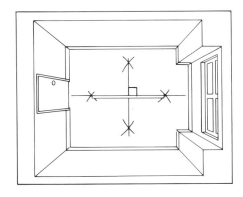

1 It is best to start from the centre of the room, so measure along to the centre of two opposite walls and snap a chalk line across the floor. Now mark the centre-point of the line and loose-lay one or two of the tiles out at right angles to the line. Use these to provide a point at which you can snap a bisecting line at right angles to the first.

Place a loose row of tiles along each line and check that there will not be narrow pieces of tile at the doorway. It may be necessary to adjust your lines a little to suit.

Vinyl tiles are easy to handle, and can be used to create striking designs

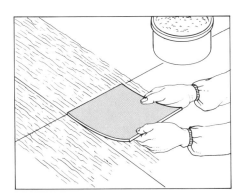

2 Apply adhesive to the floor (*see opposite page*) with a notched spreader and position your first tile so that one corner fits against the centre chalk cross. Press the tile down firmly but try not to slide it, or adhesive will rise over the edge.

Continue tiling in both directions, then, when the last whole tiles have been laid, cut the border tiles to fit.

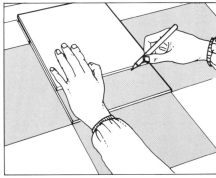

3 Place the border tile to be cut squarely on top of the last tile, then slide another tile over it until it touches the wall. Make a pencil line on the loose tile below; cut to this line, and the tile should fit exactly. Continue cutting in the same way.

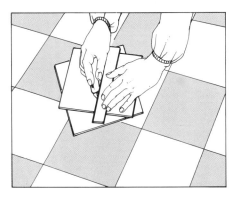

4 Cutting is best done with a straightedge and knife, working on a scrap piece of hardboard or spare tile. Do not try to cut through tiles in one pass; make a number of cuts until the knife gets through, and remember to work away from the hand holding the tile.

With small pieces of tile, it is easier to apply adhesive to the tile rather than to the floor.

AWKWARD CUTS

It is much easier to deal with awkward shapes when working with tiles, as you can complete the main body of tiling then tackle difficult areas piece by piece. Use a knife, or in small areas difficult to negotiate switch to scissors.

When you are shaping individual tiles, bear in mind that any graining or pattern must run the right way. Mistakes can be wasteful. Keep spare tiles in the warm. Vinyl is easier to cut when soft – and you will find that the tiles flex more easily.

EXTERNAL CORNERS

To cut around an external corner where one tile is involved, use the basic technique described for cutting border tiles. (*See page 81, Laying Vinyl Tiles, steps 3 and 4.*)

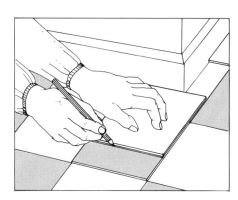

1 Place two full tiles over the last full tile and slide the top tile over to lie against the skirting edge. Mark a line on the under-tile.

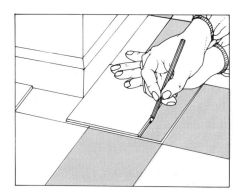

2 Now carefully move the under tile and the tile on top of it around the corner, without turning them, and place over a full tile. Mark a line on

the lower tile as you did in the previous step. You will now have a marked rectangular shape.

3 Cut out the rectangle you have marked, and glue the tile in place.

UNUSUAL SHAPES

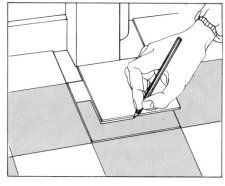

1 To cut around an awkward shape, place the tile to be cut on a last full tile. Place a second tile on top. Slide the top tile against the item to be cut around. Mark the under tile.

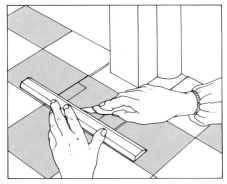

2 Move the loose tile, keeping its edges parallel with the under tile, and make a number of other marks until the shape to be cut has been

reproduced on the tile you plan to cut. Join up these marks and then cut the tile to size.

USING A TEMPLATE FORMER

Intricate shapes may also be reproduced using a template former or profile gauge, as shown in the pictures below.

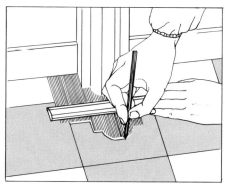

1 Line up the blades or needles on the gauge, then press them against the shape firmly enough for it to displace the gauge blades.

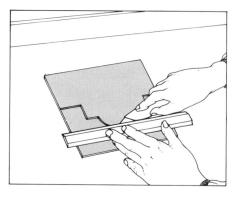

2 The tool may then be moved to the appropriate tile, and the shape drawn on it in the correct position. Cut out with a knife or scissors.

TILING AROUND A PIPE

Cut an edge tile to fit. Push it against the pipe and mark the centre. Move the tile against the wall and mark the pipe centre on the edge. Draw lines from both points and cut a hole where they bisect. Make a slit to feed around the pipe.

CARPET TILES

While you cannot get the variety of patterns available in carpet from the roll, carpet tiles have a number of advantages worth considering, especially in the kitchen and bathroom. Because you are dealing with small units they are easy to lay and, should some get worn or damaged, loose-laid tiles are easily lifted and replaced.

Most tiles have a definite pile direction, and this may be marked on the underside of each tile by means of a directional arrow. To produce a chequered effect you need to place adjoining tiles with the arrows at right angles to each other. If you want an overall smooth effect, run all the arrows (and hence the pile) the same way.

You can lay tiles over any clean, dry and smooth surface, but you may have difficulty placing them over old vinyl or a similar shiny surface as they tend to slide easily. Use a little double-sided carpet tape under the tiles to stabilize them and, if you are laying hardboard to level a timber floor, lay it with the rough side up.

Like all carpet, tiles come in a number of qualities, and it is wise to use good quality deep pile ones wherever they will be subjected to heavy wear. Cheap tiles soon flatten and even wear through, so they should only be used in utility rooms or less frequently used areas.

Never be tempted to lay tiles over uneven surfaces. The edges of the tiles will lift and be a danger, and will be pulled out of place easily. They will also wear very quickly.

As carpet tiles are designed to be butted tightly together, you can start along a wall edge as long as you will not end up with a thin sliver of tile at the far wall. Lay out a row of tiles and see how they space. If the spacing could be better, mark the floor as for vinyl tiles (*see page 81, Laying Vinyl Tiles*) and start in the middle and work out.

Left: You can use the weave of carpet tiles as well as the pile to create a design. Ideal in kitchens, they can be replaced if damaged

Above: Carpet tiles are available in a wide range of colours and textures

Below: Check the direction of the pile before laying

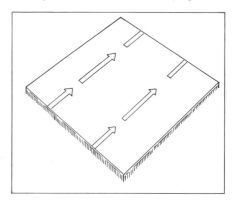

If you start at a wall, lay a row of tiles, checking the pile direction on each tile. Add your next row, pushing the tiles firmly into contact as you go. Shuffling your feet over them will help when a good number have been laid.

If you start from the room centre, stick down a few central tiles, using carpet adhesive, and wait until it sets hard. You will need to push against these central tiles to pack tiles in tightly as you work out.

Cutting carpet-tiles

Border tiles may be cut to fit in the same manner as vinyl tiles (*see page 81, Laying Vinyl Tiles*). Mark a nick with a craft knife in the edges of each tile where you want to cut a line. Turn the tile over and use a straightedge and craft knife to cut through the backing. Take this in easy stages, cutting over the line until the blade goes right through the tile. Always cut away from your holding hand.

Some tiles have a bitumen content in the base, so you will need to clean your knife blade occasionally with

white spirit in order to keep it running smoothly.

Before you cut edge tiles, go over the whole carpet, tightening up the tiles against each other. You are relying on the edge tiles to hold all

Chequerboard patterns can be created by laying adjacent carpet tiles with the pile running in opposite directions

the tiles tight, so err on the generous side when cutting.

Tiles which go into doorways will have nothing to press against so cut these tiles so they finish under the centre of the door, then fix them in place either with carpet adhesive or with double-sided carpet tape.

If carpet tiles are moved to spread wear, bear in mind the pile direction when deciding which to transpose.

Soft and luxurious, deep-pile carpet tiles will give the look and feel of a fitted carpet *if you lay them with the pile running in the same direction*

EXTRA TILES

When buying carpet tiles, invest in three or four spares to store away for future use should existing tiles get badly worn or damaged. This is most useful in kitchens and bathrooms, particularly in the former where spills may spoil tiles.

Remember manufacturers produce special grades of carpet tile for areas where spills are likely. Many of the fibres used will resist stains and most household chemicals.

FITTINGS AND FIXTURES

Probably the most satisfying part of decorating is dressing the room after you have completed the painting and papering. You want all the elements in the room to tie in together. If you have not finalized how best to stamp your own personality on the room in question, the following pages may help you. The way your curtains are hung or draped, or whether or not you have net curtains can affect the general appearance of the room. It also affects the amount of light entering, so experiment a little before making your final decision.

Curtains

Consider how much of the window wall is to be covered by curtaining and whether you want to make a feature of it. Where the windows are small, it sometimes helps to extend the curtain rail either side of the opening so that when the curtains are pulled, the full window is exposed for maximum daylight.

Do you want the rail to be hidden when the curtains are drawn? Decorative poles can enhance a window. Some incorporate a rail so that standard curtain hooks can be used.

Would the window benefit from a pelmet? Do you want to add net curtains for privacy when the main curtains are open, or do you want them draped as a feature of the window?

Blinds

Modern blinds are available in many styles. Venetian blinds tend to look best in kitchens and bathrooms, as do roller blinds. Vertical louvres can be a feature in a lounge or dining room. Draped blinds look especially effective in bedrooms for a softer touch.

Fittings

Choose from a vast range of door fittings to suit the decoration of your room, from brass to china. Lighting is important: wall lights, room lights and warm, coloured lamps can affect the whole mood of the room. Keep fluorescent lighting in the kitchen or bathroom, where strong light is desirable.

CURTAIN STYLING

Drape curtains to hide an unpleasant view

Frame a blind with curtains and a pelmet

Here fabric has been cleverly draped and tied along the length of a pelmet

Curtain style can greatly influence the impact of a room. A wall with one or two small windows can become a feature if you hang floor-length curtains along the entire length of the room, while large windows provide an opportunity to drape curtains.

Right: *Cut a curved top from plywood and screw this to three battens attached to the top and sides of the frame. Fix an easily-curved aluminium track to the curved edge of the board*

Use a jig saw to cut out the curved edge of a decorative pelmet

SHEER STYLING

Sheers can be styled in much the same way as curtains, and also used for gathered and pleated blinds. They provide daytime privacy, but at night you will need to draw the curtains, release a blind or close shutters so that the room is not on view from outside when lights go on.

Old lace is best hung flat to show off the intricate design. Add interest to plain nets with a frill of decorative lace sewn along the lower edge. To show off plants or ornaments on a sill, use nets with an arched hem.

Above: In a deep alcove or above a work surface use a roller blind which pulls up out of the way when not in use
Right: A lace panel is ideally hung where it will not pick up too much dirt

Lengths of lace-edged net can be draped attractively to form a valance

Drape sheer curtains but keep some of the view, using cord for tie backs

With sheer main curtains, include a venetian blind for privacy at night

TRACKS AND POLES

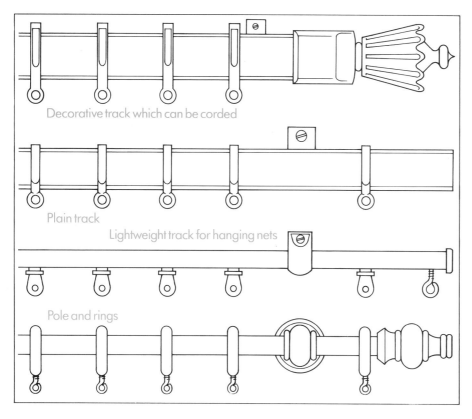

Decorative track which can be corded

Plain track

Lightweight track for hanging nets

Pole and rings

Fixing a rail to the wall can be quite difficult where there is a lintel of reinforced concrete or steel covered with plaster. If you find drilling difficult, it is better to screw a batten to the wall and secure the rail to it with shorter screws. Do not reduce the number of holding brackets – especially when hanging heavy curtains. The weight of the curtains can distort the track.

Many tracks may also be screwed to the ceiling to provide a full-length curtain drop. You must, however, have something substantial to screw into. A thickness of ceiling plaster is not enough. If you are unable to find a suitable joist, you need to lay timber between joists – and to do this you need access from above.

Track types

Tracks are available mainly in PVC or aluminium. Both are strong, but aluminium is easiest to form to tight curves or awkward shapes.

Visible sliders The simplest type of rail has sliders which clip over the rail and move along.
Smooth rail Here, the sliders are inserted into grooves on the back of the track, or into a recess below it.
Cording sets Most types of rail have a matching cording set which enables the curtains to be opened or closed by cord. Unless you are familiar with cording, install the set before you put the rail up to see how it works. This is easier at this stage than when the rail is up.
Valance rails These are available for many tracks. A pelmet can be mounted in front of the curtain heading. (*See page 90, Pelmets.*)
Poles Available in timber, timber and brass, or brass only, poles can be an attractive feature of a window. On some types, curtains are hung from rings which slide on the pole, while on the more sophisticated types, rings slide within the pole.

Wherever possible, screw the holding brackets direct to the wall as battens look clumsy. Treat tracks regularly with grease-free lubricant for smooth running.

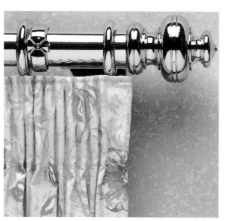

Above: Modern tapes offer a choice of pockets for hooks, enabling you to position the heading to hide a track, left, or hang below a rail, above

Left: If you cover a curtain heading with a pelmet or valance, you can hang curtains below the track, as the top will be hidden from view

TAPES AND HOOKS

It is important to decide what kind of heading you want your curtains to have. This will determine how the top of the curtain will pleat and form folds, and whether the curtain will hang below the track, or in such a way that the curtain hides the track completely when the curtains are drawn.

Some pleating can be done by hand, but the simplest way is to choose a heading tape which can give you the required pleating. Matching the tape will be particular types of hook, which lock into the tape and provide a connection to the track. On simple systems, the hooks may be of tough plastic but in the more complex systems, the hooks are of metal. There are many variations of heading, but here are a few of the more common ones.

Gathered heading The simple gathering tape is mainly used for curtains which will be hidden behind a pelmet or valance. The gathering may be evenly distributed or clustered, and can be controlled by adjusting the draw-cords.

Pencil pleating This is formed by using stiffened tape in one of a number of widths. There is a choice of pockets for hooks, depending on

Curtain tape forms the folds in a valance

Pencil pleats for use with a pole or track

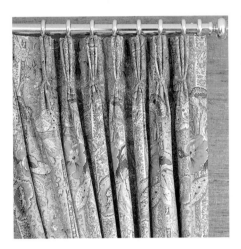

Spaced triple pleating for thicker fabrics

Pencil pleats head an Austrian blind

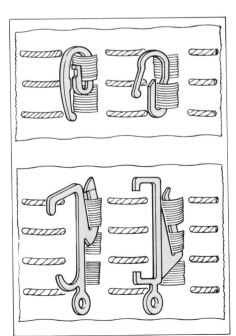

__Left:__ Small hooks, above, are suitable for hanging nets, and can be slotted into the loops of main curtain hooks, below

whether you want the curtain to hang below or cover the track.

Triple pleating Sometimes called pinch pleating, this effect is achieved by use of a stiffened tape which pulls up to form groups of pleats with spaces between. Some tapes need special hooks to support the pleats. The curtain may hang below or cover the track.

Cartridge pleating Special split hooks are used to keep the regular row of pleats formed with this tape, and it is quite common to stuff the tops of the pleats with cotton wool or tissue paper to help retain their rounded shape.

HANGING NETS

Lightweight versions of most of the tapes described on this page are available for hanging nets. Sometimes it is sufficient simply to machine a pocket near the head of the net and insert a lightweight rod or plastic-coated curtain wire.

Screw an eyelet into each end of the rod. Pull the rod tight, and support it with two rustproof eyelets screwed into the window frame.

Where the width exceeds 1 metre (yd), you may need a supporting pin in the centre of the frame to reduce sag.

MAKING A PELMET

A pelmet serves three main functions. It can form an attractive window feature; it hides an exposed curtain rail and it keeps the head of the curtains and the track clean.

The illustration shows how to make a simple pelmet, designed to locate over two steel pins (screws with the heads taken off with a mini hacksaw). Drill screw holes, and plug and screw the holding batten to the wall, positioned so that it represents the top of the pelmet less the thickness of piece A.

Drilling can be difficult if you encounter a reinforced concrete lintel. Use a power drill with hammer action and a sharp masonry drill.

Assembling the pelmet

With all of the lengths cut to size and smoothed with glass paper, glue and pin them together. Having inserted two screws into the wall batten, cut off the heads immediately under the countersink. Offer the pelmet to the batten, and tap it with a hammer to make indentations where the pins are located. Drill holes in the pelmet top so that the pelmet slips over the pins.

To shape a pelmet edge, before assembly make a pattern half the width of the front board, trace and flip it over to trace the other side. Cut out with a jig saw. Either paint the pelmet, or cover it with matching fabric.

Fabric pelmets may be made from stiffened material, or frilled or pleated curtain material mounted on a valance rail. A valance rail clips in front of a curtain track, on to which you can hook the pelmet. The valance may be straight, or curved to fit around a bay window. Check when choosing your track whether a matching valance is available.

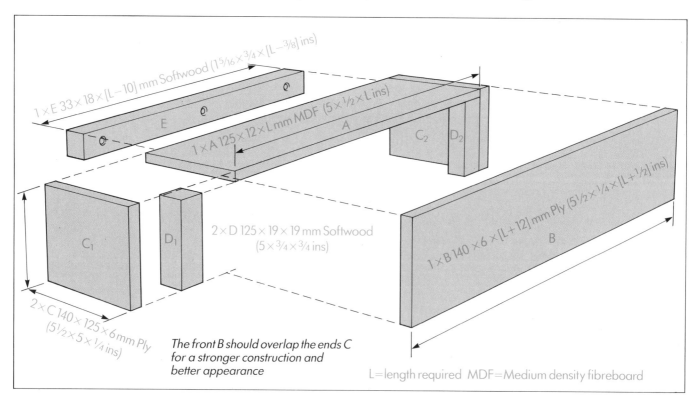

1 × E 33 × 18 × [L−10] mm Softwood (1⁵⁄₁₆ × ³⁄₄ × [L−³⁄₈] ins)

1 × A 125 × 12 × L mm MDF (5 × ¹⁄₂ × L ins)

1 × B 140 × 6 × [L+12] mm Ply (5¹⁄₂ × ¹⁄₄ × [L+¹⁄₂] ins)

2 × D 125 × 19 × 19 mm Softwood (5 × ³⁄₄ × ³⁄₄ ins)

2 × C 140 × 125 × 6 mm Ply (5¹⁄₂ × 5 × ¹⁄₄ ins)

The front B should overlap the ends C for a stronger construction and better appearance

L=length required MDF=Medium density fibreboard

TYPES OF BLIND

Left: Roman blinds fold up in small pleats
Above: Roller blinds, ideal for small windows

Austrian blinds form softly-pleated scallops

Vertical slat blinds, best for large windows

Horizontal louvres are ideal for kitchens

Blinds are less expensive to buy than curtains because far less material is involved. They roll up out of the way, leaving worktops clear, and can let in more light than drawn-back curtains – unless the curtains have been arranged to pull back completely clear of a window. They can often be bought ready-made, made to order or built from a kit. The main types are as follows.

Roller blind This is probably the cheapest of the blinds.
Roman blind This works by pull-cords and, while it may look similar to a roller blind when down, it pulls up into attractive pleats.
Austrian blind This is a sophisticated form of Roman blind. It pulls up into soft frills.
Venetian blind Commonly used in kitchens and bathrooms, this blind consists of a number of slats which can be angled and raised by cord-control. The slats need to be kept clean – especially in locations like the kitchen.

With the vertical-slat venetian blind, a simple mechanism allows you to angle slats and let in a little light, or close the slats completely.
Festoon blind Often of a silky fabric, it falls in scalloped folds.

LEADED LIGHTS AND STAINED GLASS

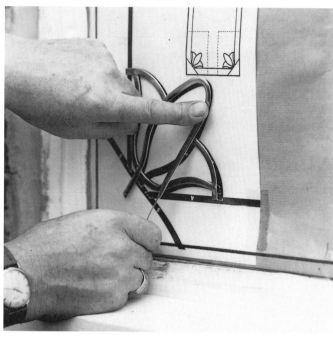

Above: A leading kit for adding pattern to a plain window. Tape it behind the glass

Right: For leaded lights, apply self-adhesive leading strips in a diagonal pattern

Far right: Copy stained glass using a kit or employ a specialist

Leaded lights

Leaded lights are made up of small pieces of glass set in H-shaped lead strips or cames. Making up such panels is a skilled job best left to the professional, but effective imitations can be made using self-adhesive lead strip, available in kits.

Leading can be applied to both sides of the glass, and the best time to do it is when reglazing. It is easier to apply if glass is laid flat.

First make an accurate pattern from which to work. Choose the largest pane of glass you will be decorating, and cut a sheet of brown paper the exact size of the glass. Mark out your pattern in squares or diamonds so that the spacing of the lines is balanced.

Clean the glass thoroughly to remove all grease and grime and keep your fingers off the surface.

Put the paper pattern over the glass, unless it is in situ, and tape the pattern behind the glass.

Separate the lead strips and pull each taut to remove any wrinkles, then apply one strip along a guideline, making sure it is straight and true before smoothing firmly. Continue building up the pattern. Remove the paper pattern when the leading is complete and repeat the procedure on the other side, carefully matching the strips.

Stained glass

If you have existing leaded lights or stained-glass panels, keep them in good condition. There are specialist companies which will supply you with all the materials necessary to construct your own leaded lights. Others will carry out work to your instructions. Commissioning work can be expensive, however. A simple design in ornamental leaded light for a door panel 60 cm × 60 cm (24 in × 24 in) could cost you twice as much as a good hardwood door. Stained-glass panels are usually hand-painted then fired, with a view to being incorporated into an area of leaded light.

WAYS WITH MIRRORS

Mirrors may be used to direct light into darkened areas, or to multiply the amount of light available. (*See also page 11, Mirror Magic.*) Where semi-basement rooms receive little daylight, mirrors may be used to direct light into the room. Sheet mirror on the walls of a skylight well will vastly increase the amount of light in the area below. Be careful to attach the mirror panels firmly to the wall with screws. A thin rim of wood nailed or glued to the base of the skylight will help give support to the panels.

Foliage can be enhanced by mirrors. Mosaic mirror tiles, used as part of a fire surround, will enhance the effect of foliage from any plants or ferns standing in front of it.

An alcove lends itself to mirror tiles or mosaic, especially when combined with spotlights, which will bounce the light. As sheet mosaic is flexible, it may be fitted around pillars or to the curve of an alcove, breaking the light into patterns.

Mirrors are available in a number of subtle shades which may also be used to add mood and soften colours in a room. Large expanses of mirror glass can be made more interesting if they are engraved.

When choosing mirrors for kitchens and bathrooms, check that they are damp-resistant.

Above: *Sheets of mirror covering a wall will double the apparent room size*

Top: *Increase the light in a dark room with mirrors on a wall at right angles to a main window. Here light sparkles on glassware*

Above: *Mirror panels provide decoration for flush doors and draw light through to the area beyond; or use mirror mosaic*

Right: *A narrow hall appears far wider if mirror is used on a long wall. Show off wall decorations to enhance the effect*

GLOSSARY OF TERMS

In the course of decorating or employing a tradesman, you may come across various terms, some familiar and some not so. The following is a guide to some of the most common DIY names and terms:

Aggregates
The ingredients of concrete. Usually stone or gravel, and sand.

Architrave
A timber moulding around an internal door frame.

Barge board
A timber edge-piece covering a gable end.

Batten
A small section of timber.

Beading
Small section of decorative timber often used to hide a gap.

Casement window
One which is hinged at the side.

Casing
The lining of an internal door.

Caulking
Used for sealing joins between tiles and the edge of a bath, shower or sink.

Cavity (stud) walls
A wall consisting of two leaves of brick, or brick and block, to leave an air space between.

Ceiling joist
The timbers supporting the ceiling.

Chinagraph pencil
Special pencil that can write on hard, smooth surfaces like china, glass, tiles and so on.

Concrete raft
A form of house foundation often associated with weak ground.

Conduit
A small pipe for housing electric wiring.

Countersink
To make a wide, shallow hole in timber to take the head of a countersunk head screw. This is sometimes covered with filler so that the fixing is completely hidden.

Damp proof course
An impervious horizontal barrier in a wall to prevent the passage of damp.

Distemper
Old fashioned water-based paint which is hard to remove.

Drip groove
A channel cut along the underside of a window sill or weatherboard to shed rainwater.

Dry lining
Plasterboard finish for a wall, as opposed to wet plastering.

Eaves
Lower edge of a roof where the roof extends out from the wall.

Escutcheon
Keyhole cover plate.

Fascia
The horizontal board below the roof which carries the gutters.

Fillet
Infill piece to cover a small gap.

Flashing
This is the material used to bridge a gap between two surfaces – such as between chimney and roof.

Flaunching
Mortar filling around the bases of chimney pots.

Flush door
A smooth-faced door with no panels.

Glazing beads
Small strips which are used to hold glass in place.

Grounds
Timber blocks set in a wall to which skirting boards are nailed.

Grout
Material for filling joints between tiles.

Hanger
A metal support for holding joist ends.

Hardcore
Broken brick or stone used for firming foundations.

Hopper
Open, funnel-like fitting on a drainpipe.

Jamb
Vertical side-member of window or door frame.

Joist
Timber supporting floor or ceiling.

Lath
This is a small wood strip. Laths are used in older walls and ceilings for supporting plaster.

Lintel
A support above a door or window of concrete, steel or timber.

Microporous
The description of a paint or varnish which is able to 'breathe' without allowing damp in.

Mortice lock
A lock which is built into the thickness of the door, and one of the more secure types of lock.

Mullion
This is the vertical central member of a window frame (see also Jamb).

Newel
Structural post of a staircase.

Nogging
Horizontal strengthening piece in a stud frame.

Parging
The cement lining to a flue.

Pitched roof
Roof sloping more than 20° from the horizontal.

Pivot-hung window
Window which swings on its axis.

Pointing
Mortar finishing joints between bricks.

Profile gauge
See Template Former

Purlin
Longitudinal timber linking rafters in a roof.

Rafter
Timber supporting the roof covering.

Rail
Horizontal member of a door or window.

Rendering
Coating on an internal or external wall surface.

Reveal
Internal side surface of a recess.

Ridge board
Horizontal timber supporting the ridge of a roof.

Ridge tiles
Top row of tiles on a roof forming a seal.

Riser
Vertical part of a step or stair.

Rising butt
Hinge which enables a door to rise over a carpet.

Sash window
One which opens and shuts by having units which slide up and down.

Screed
A thin layer applied to level a solid floor.

Shiplap
A type of overlapping boarding used externally. Traditionally of timber, it may now also be made of plastic.

Shoe
The fitting at the foot of a rainwater pipe.

Soffit
An exposed under-surface, such as on a lintel.

Sole plate
The base timber of a stud frame, secured to the floor.

Spacing nibs
Small projections on either side of a tile.

Sprig
Small pin used to hold glass before putty is added.

Stile
The vertical frame member of a door or window.

String
The side member of a staircase into which treads and risers fit.

Stud frame
System of building a partition by using heavy vertical timbers with cross-timbers which are then clad.

Template former
Otherwise known as a profile gauge, this is a comb-like tool for reproducing the shapes of doorframes or pipes. The steel pins or teeth follow the shape of the object. The exact shape can then be transferred to the floorcovering with a pencil, and cut out.

Threshold strip
The metal strip which holds down a floorcovering in a doorway.

Tile spacers
Plastic cross-shaped spacers which fit into the corners of tiles. They are left in place and grouted over, and are used instead of spacing nibs.

Transome
Horizontal member of a window frame.

Tread
Horizontal board of step or stair.

Valley
The meeting point of two pitched roofs where water will drain off.

Wall plate
A timber fixed horizontally to a wall, to which joists and rafters are nailed.

Wall tie
A metal fitting designed to hold two sections of masonry together.

Weatherboard
A sloping section on the base of an outside door to direct rainwater away from the door.

Window board
An interior timber window sill.

Window stay
A bar which is designed to hold a window open.

INDEX

A

adhesives 36, 38, 80
aerosol cans, paint in 30
alloy frames 54
anti-condensation paint 28
archways, papering 66

B

barge boards 46
blinds 85, 91
blistering in wallpapers 64
blowtorches 43
brickwork 44, 46, 53
brushes 12, 18-19, 20, 22, 49, 50, 57

C

carpet tiles 37, 83-4
ceilings:
    calculating rolls of paper for 34
    finished effects 33
    'lowering' 11
    painting 48
    preparation 40, 42
    tiles/tiling 37, 70
    wallpapering 58, 59-60
cellulose paints 21
ceramic tiles 37
chemical stripping 43
chimney stacks 44
cladding 45, 56
clamps 15
cleaners 37, 38
colour 8-9
concrete floors 76-7
cording sets, curtain 88
cork 29, 33, 37, 63
corners, dealing with 39, 65, 80, 82
coverage of paint 29
coveralls 26
coving 41, 50
creases in wallpaper, removing 63
creosote 20, 30
cripples 24, 52
curtains 85, 86-9
cutting tiles 36, 72

D

damp 31, 46
dash finishes, exterior 46, 53
distemper brushes 20
doors:
    door fittings 85
    exterior maintenance 45
    exterior painting 54
    painting 51
    papering round 66
    preparation 29, 40
    trimming vinyl round 79-80
downpipes 55
drilling tiles 73
duplex paper 32, 42
dusting brushes 20

E

easy-strip coverings 31
embossed wallcoverings 12, 32, 33
emergency kits 26
emulsion paints 18, 19, 28, 50

enamels 28
exterior painting 52-7

F

fabrics 10, 85-7
face masks 26, 43
fascia boards 46
fillers 38, 47
fireplaces 67
flashings 44
flock 33
flooring 37, 76-84
foil wallcoverings 63
frames 40
friezes 68
fungicides 38

G

glass cutters 16
gloves 26
glue guns 16
goggles 21, 26
grasscloth 33
grouting tiles 36, 73
guttering 44, 55

H

hammers 16
heat-resistant paint 29
hessian 33, 42, 63
hiring equipment 25
hooks, curtain 89
hot air guns 43

I

imitation effects 12

K

knives 15, 22
knots, treating, in timber 54

L

lacquer paints 28
ladders 23, 24, 25
lavatories, papering round 67
lead danger 43
leaded lights 92
light fittings 40, 60
light switches 50, 65
lighting 8, 12, 85
Lincrusta, stripping 42
lining paper 32

M

masks 21, 26, 43
masonry paints 20, 29
metal paints 28, 53, 54
microporous paints 28
mirrors 11, 93
mosaic tiles 36
motifs, wallcovering 68

N

nets 87, 89
Novamura 32, 62

P

pads, paint 20, 49, 50
paint kettles 18, 49
painting 48-57
    ceiling tiles 37
    surface preparation 39-40, 42, 43, 45, 47

tools for 18-21
    see also paints
paints 28-30
    textured 12, 29
    see also painting
papering see wallpapering
parquet 37
pasting tables 22
pattern 10-11
pebbledash 46
pedestal basins, laying vinyl round 80
pelmets 90
picture rails 40, 50
pincers 15, 72
pipes, tiling round 82
plasterboard 39
plastic cladding 56
platforms 23, 24, 25, 48
pleating curtains 85
pliers 15
poles, curtain 88
power tools 14, 15, 17
preparation 27, 39-47
protective clothing 26
putties 38

R

radiators 19, 28, 67
rags 18
ready-pasted wallpaper 31, 60-1
recesses, papering 65
relief wallcoverings 12, 32, 33
rendering 46
rollers 12, 19, 22, 48, 49, 50
roof maintenance 29, 44
rulers 15
rust resistant finishes 28

S

safety 7, 21, 23, 24, 26, 52, 78
sanders 17
saws 15, 72
scaffolds 23, 24
scrapers, flexible 18
screwdrivers 15
sealants, bathroom 74
seams in wallcoverings 32
shave hooks 18
sheers 87
shower cabinets, tiling, 74
silk wallcoverings 33, 63
size (powder/paste) 58
skin on paint 57
skin protection 26
skirting boards 40, 50
slips, brick/stone 12
solid emulsion paints 19, 48
solid floors 76
spanners 16
spirit levels 16
spashbacks, tiling 74
spray guns 17, 21
stained glass 92
stains, ceiling 40
stairwells 52
staple guns 16
steam strippers 40, 42
stencils for friezes 68
stepladders 23, 24
stonework 53
storage 16, 50
stripping 40, 42-3

switches, light 50, 65

T

tapes, curtain heading 89
template formers 72, 82
texture 12, 29
tiles 35-7
    carpet 83-4
    laying vinyl 81-2
    red paint 28
    tiled floors 76-7
    tiling 69-75
timber see wood
tool belts 26
tools 7, 14-27
tracks, curtain 88
trestles 24

V

valance rails 88
varnishes 29
vinyl:
    floor coverings 37, 78-82
    wallcoverings 12, 32, 33, 42, 64

W

wall lights 12
wall tiles 35-6
wallcoverings 31-3
    patterned 10
    stripping 42
    textured 12
    see also wallpapering
wallpapering 58-68
    behind fittings 27
    calculating rolls required 34
    surface preparation 39, 42
    tools for 22
    See also wallcoverings
walls:
    exterior maintenance 46
    exterior painting 52-3
    painting 49
    papering 62-7
    preparation 39
    tiles/tiling 35-6, 71
windows:
    exterior maintenance 45
    exterior painting 53
    painting 51
    preparation 29, 40
wood:
    cladding 56
    preserving/repairing 30, 47
    timber floors 77
    window frames 53
wood chip wallcoverings 12
workbenches 15
worktops, tiling 75